Beginner's
WELSH

Heini Gruffudd

HIPPOCRENE BOOKS
New York

I'm plant

Efa, Nona, Gwydion ac Anna

Gwlad heb iaith, gwlad heb galon

Cataloging-in-Publication Data available from Library of Congress.

Copyright © 1998 Heini Gruffudd
All rights reserved.

For information, address:
HIPPOCRENE BOOKS, INC.
171 Madison Avenue
New York, NY 10016

ISBN 0-7818-0589-9

Printed in the United States of America.

TABLE OF CONTENTS

INTRODUCTION

The Welsh language, and its rich culture and heritage, have survived successfully to the end of the twentieth century, in spite of having to compete with its large neighbor, English. More than half a million people speak Welsh, some 20% of the total population of 2,750,000, and they are spread fairly equally numerically throughout the country.

Many people come to Britain not knowing that Wales exists, or that a different language has been spoken here for 1,600 years. Fewer still realize that Welsh, or old Welsh, and its ancestor, 'Brythoneg', or 'Britannic', was the language spoken over most of the territory of Britain before the English had thought of coming here. Today Welsh as a spoken language is more or less limited to Wales, but there are communities of Welsh speakers in many parts of the world including Patagonia, and the United States, where there were a quarter of a million Welsh speakers at the end of the 19th century. Many thousands of Welsh speakers also moved to English cities e.g. Liverpool and London.

In Wales, however, beginning in the middle of the 19th century, the circumstances governing the use of language were largely damaging to the future of Welsh. English was the only language of law and administration; in the latter half of that century Welsh was banned in schools. In spite of this a national resurgence has seen Welsh gaining ground once again. A quarter of Wales' primary schools are Welsh medium schools. Welsh is now taught as a subject in almost all schools in Wales, and there are Welsh language channels, both on radio and television. Welsh literature, which has an unbroken tradition going back to 600 AD, is flourishing.

Knowing Welsh, therefore, is the key to getting a first hand experience of Welsh history and literature. But for the casual visitor, it is also the key to ensure a warm welcome in many parts of Wales, as Welsh is still the first language of the most beautiful parts of the country in west and north Wales.

This book has two parts. The first gives you information about the country (geography, history, economy, culture, fate of the language, customs and traditions), while the second part consists of language lessons.

The language lessons are designed for a traveller or a non-specialist. You will learn useful phrases and words for special situations as well as basic grammar hints. The lessons will not cover all grammatical problems, nor will they give a rich vocabulary for sophisticated conversation. Nevertheless they will teach you enough to feel comfortable in a variety of situations, and enough to ensure you are a welcome guest, as the Welsh show great affinity for those interested in their language and culture.

We hope that with this small, compact book you will have in your pocket a collection of bits of information, sufficient to carry out satisfying conversations with the people of the country you visit, in their own language. Several U.S. universities teach Welsh, and Cymdeithas Madog organizes a week long Welsh course annually in the States. Welsh speakers and Welsh lessons are available on the internet. For courses in Wales contact Welsh for Adults Organiser, WJEC, 245 Western Ave., Cardiff. We wish you good luck in your study and a wonderful trip.

Beginner's
WELSH

CYMRU
WALES

Caergybi
Holyhead

Ynys Môn
Anglesey

Llandudno

Rhyl

Conwy

Bangor

Fflint
Flint

Caernarfon

Wrecsam
Wrexham

▲ Yr Wyddfa
Snowdon

Bala

LLOEGR
ENGLAND

▲ Aran

Dolgellau

▲ Cader Idris

● Machynlleth

Bae Ceredigion
Cardigan Bay

Y Drenewydd
Newtown

Aberystwyth

▲ Pumlumon

Môr Iwerddon
Irish Sea

● Aberaeron

Abergwaun
Fishguard

Aberteifi
Cardigan

● Llanbedr
Lampeter

Aberhonddu
Brecon

▲ Preseli

Caerfyrddin
Carmarthen

Bannau Brycheiniog ▲
Brecon Beacons

● Tŷ Ddewi
St. David's

Penfro
Pembroke

Merthyr Tudful
Merthyr Tydfil

Castell-nedd

Abertawe
Swansea

Neath

Y Rhondda

Casnewydd
Newport

Caerffili
Caerphilly ●

Port Talbot

Môr Hafren
Bristol Channel

Caerdydd
Cardiff

GEOGRAPHY

Wales is a small country situated to the west of England, and over the sea from Ireland. Its surface area is 20,767 sq. km (8,016 sq. miles) and it has a population of 2,800,000 inhabitants. Administratively, Wales has a national assembly[1], which decides on matters of home interest, e.g. education, the economy, health and welfare, but otherwise it sends 40 M.P.s to the London Parliament. In local government, Wales is divided into 22 local government authorities.

The country is largely hilly and mountainous. The only lowland areas are the south and north Wales coastal strips, and the island of Anglesey in North Wales. 81% of the country is in agricultural use, 12% woodland, and 7% urban.

The country has several mountain ranges: Snowdonia in the north-west, where Snowdon (3,560 ft.) is the highest mountain. Snowdonia has 15 peaks over 3,000 ft. The Cambrian Mountains cover much of mid Wales, to the east of the seaside and university town of Aberystwyth, and the Brecon Beacons have the highest mountain in South Wales (Pen y fan, 2,907 ft.). Other ranges include the Preseli hills in Pembrokeshire, southwest Wales, the Clwydian hills in north-east Wales, and the Black mountains of Gwent in south-east Wales. If the territory of Wales were spread flat, the country would be four times its size!

Wales has a beautiful coastline to its north, west and south, and is linked to England along its eastern border. The coastline has a total of 732 miles, and forms 17 per cent of the total British coastline. The longest river is the Severn (220 miles) which runs from its source in the Cambrian mountains eastwards to England before flowing back along the South Wales Coast

---

[1] Setting up date 1999 after the Welsh voted for establishing it in an historic referendum on 18 September 1997.

through the Bristol Channel (called 'Môr Hafren' in Welsh - the Severn Sea). There are good fishing rivers flowing towards the sea in west and south Wales, the Tywi (68 miles) (flowing through Carmarthen in the south) and Teifi (73 miles) (flowing through Cardigan) in the west. Other rivers flowing partly through England but originating in Wales are Dee (111 miles), flowing to the sea at the border of Wales and England in the north, and Wye (130 miles) which forms the south-eastern border of Wales. There are 20 rivers longer than 25 miles, and a total of around 15,000 miles of river.

The country has more than 400 natural lakes and 90 reservoirs. Llyn Tegid, near Bala in north-west Wales, 1.69 sq. miles, is the largest natural lake. Others in mid and north Wales are reservoirs, supplying English cities with cheap water. This has long been a bone of contention, as has been the drowning of Welsh communities. These lakes include Llyn Celyn, Vyrnwy, Claerwen and Clywedog. Lake Brianne in the mountains of southern mid Wales supplies water for Swansea and the surrounding area.

The country is fairly sparsely populated, except for the industrial areas of south-east and north-east Wales. These areas were for two hundred years centers of heavy industry, with coal iron, steel and copper production supplying much of the early wealth and power of the British Empire. In the twentieth century the number of coal miners fell from a quarter of a million to a few thousand, and many large steel works closed. These industries have to some extent been replaced by electronic factories, producing T.V. sets and computer materials, and by factories producing parts for motor cars.

Some areas, including parts of the main holiday areas of north and west Wales, have been inundated by English people, buying up homes at the expense of the local people. At the turn of the twentieth century scores of thousands of English people, and some from other countries, came to Wales to work in the

10

heavy industries, but most of these have become assimilated and consider themselves Welsh.

Major cities: Cardiff (279,000 inhabitants), Swansea (182,000), Newport (133,000), Wrexham (115,000), Neath (65,000). The south-eastern valleys, including the towns of Rhondda, Pontypridd, Maesteg, Merthyr Tydfil and Aberdare have a population of more than half a million.

National parks:
Wales has three large areas of national parks: Snowdonia (838 sq. miles), Pembrokeshire Coast (225 sq. miles) and Brecon Beacons (519 sq. miles). There are 32 Country Parks which are distributed all over the country, and there are five areas of outstanding natural beauty. Among these are Gower, near Swansea, the first area to be so designated in Britain (1956). Large tracts of coastline are also protected, and Heritage Coast areas form more than 40% of the Welsh coast. There are 49 National Nature Reserves, and 19 Local Nature Reserves.

Climate: Wales has a mild climate, without extremes of heat or cold except on the highest mountains. The country has an annual rainfall of around 54 inches. Rain can fall at any time, but it is warmer in summer!   Snow does not last long in winter (except for around 100 days a year on the mountains of Snowdonia). The average July temperature is around 16°, but in summer temperatures higher than 20° Celsius occur regularly. The Gulf stream from South America keeps the South Wales coast free from frost in winter, and the sea can by comfortably bathed in in summer months.

HISTORY AND POLITICS

Welsh history can be said to start in the year 383, when Magnus Maximus, the Roman ruler, left the country with his armies in the hope of becoming the Roman Emperor. Nevertheless, the seed of Wales had already been sown in the prehistoric era.

Standing stones, dolmens and stone circles, which dot the countryside, belong to the same period as Stonehenge in England, the stones of which came from the Preseli mountains in Pembrokeshire. These stone formations, many of which were burial places, others possibly places of religious significance, were built during the pre-Celtic era. Wales consisted of people who had wandered from the Iberian peninsula, i.e. Spain and southern Europe. The Celts, who had inhabited parts of central Europe around Austria, conquered many parts of Europe, and took over Rome around 300 BC. They arrived in Britain in several waves from around 800 BC. It was their language and culture which became the languages of the present day Celtic nations. Welsh (Wales), Breton (Brittany) and Cornish (Cornwall) belong to one branch of these languages, while Irish (Ireland), Gaelic (Scotland) and Manx (Isle of Man) belong to the other.

Between the 4th and 6th centuries AD, Welsh monks preached the Gospel and established churches in many parts of Wales, Ireland, Cornwall and Brittany. At that time the Welsh were being conquered in England, while the first Welsh poetry which has survived was written around 600AD in northern England and southern Scotland. This poetry describes Welsh warriors who were defeated in battle. The historic Arthur was probably a Welsh army leader who had considerable success fighting the Anglo Saxons during this period.

The English kings of the period were anxious to consolidate their gains in England, and one of them, Offa, built an early version of the iron curtain when he built a wall, Offa's Dyke,

12

around 780AD to keep the Welsh from his kingdom. This dyke has remained more or less the border between Wales and England until today.

From 400 to 1282 the Welsh developed their own system of rulers. Among the earliest was Maelgwn Gwynedd, who ruled in north-west Wales until his death of a plague in 549. Although the country was not often united under one specific ruler, it was united by a common language and literature, a system of laws, codified by king Hywel Dda around 900AD, and by the common struggle against persistent invaders. Among the kings and princes who united most of the country under their control were Rhodri Mawr (ruled 844-878), the grand-father of Hywel Dda (c900-950), and Gruffydd ap Llywelyn (1039-63).

The invaders included Irish, Danes, Vikings and Norman English. The Normans succeeded in gaining large parts of the country, and Wales' two last great rulers included Llywelyn Fawr (the Great) (1218-40) and Llywelyn ap Gruffudd (Llywelyn II, or the Last) (1246-1282). Two wars of independence were fought, 1267-77 and 1282-83.

Most of the castles (e.g. Harlech, Caernarfon, Conwy, Beaumares in the north and Caerphilly, Cardiff, Kidwelly in the south), which are still a part of Wales' landscape, were built by the Normans, although some (e.g. Dolbadarn and Dolwyddelan in the north and Dinefwr and Dryslwyn in the south) are of Welsh origin.

The following years were ones of harsh English revenge, but under Owain Glyndŵr the Welsh regained their independence for a brief period from 1400 onwards. After his defeat, the Welsh once again thought that they had won a great victory when Henry VII, of half Welsh descent, defeated the English king at the battle of Bosworth, 1485, with the help of a Welsh army. This led, nervertheless, to the eventual political annexation of Wales by England with the Acts of Annexation of 1536 and 1542. English from now on was to be the only language of law and administration. Welsh laws were replaced by English laws, and the Welsh system of government was to become part of the English system.

It was fortunate for the Welsh language, still spoken as the only language by around 95% of the population, that in its attempt to create a united Protestant state, the English parliament called for a translation of the Bible and other religious texts into Welsh. This led in future centuries to several mass education movements, so that by the 19th century, Wales was a Welsh speaking, literate country, where the language flourished.

During the 18th and 19th centuries, nonconformist denominations flourished, taking the place of the established Protestant state church as the main religious organisation. These denominations used mainly Welsh and were part of a democratic folk culture, whereas the state church was linked to the ruling landowning and English orientated classes.

Heavy industries, including quarrying, iron and coal changed the face of many parts of the country in the nineteenth century. The valleys of South Wales became heavily populated, and at first attracted Welsh speakers from rural areas. It has been argued that this industrialisation kept most Welsh people in their own country, and thus safeguarded the language, at a time when there was mass emigration from Europe to America.

When voting rights were given generally to men in the second half of the 19th century, Wales turned its back on the English Conservative party, and was a stronghold for the Liberal Party, which advocated Welsh home rule. One of its leaders, David Lloyd George, became Prime Minister of Britain, and introduced social measures such as state pensions.

During this period of national revival, several national Welsh institutions were established, such as the University of Wales

(1893), the National Library of Wales (1907) and the National Museum of Wales (1907). Throughout the twentieth century, the cultural, economic and political life of Wales came to be organised more on more on national lines.

With the growth of heavy industries, the Labour Party grew in strength in Wales, and became the main party in Wales after the First World War. Unfortunately, until fairly recently, it only paid lip service to Welsh national aspirations, and this led to the formation of Plaid Cymru (1925), the national party of Wales whose aim is self-government for Wales. Yr Urdd, the Welsh League of Youth, which has become one of Europe's main youth movements, had already been established in 1922.

Since the Second World War there have been many important developments which are contributing to Welsh nationhood. Among these are the establishment of the Welsh Office (1964), Welsh Books Council (1961), The Welsh Playgroup Movement (1971), Welsh Development Agency (1976) and S4C (the Welsh Television Channel) (1982).

In the general election of 1997, 34 of Wales' 40 M.P.s were Labour Party M.P.s, 4 Plaid Cymru (Welsh national party), 2 Liberal, and no Conservative.

ECONOMICS

Wales was in the 19th century a center of world importance for several industries. But the history of industry in Wales is long. Copper and gold were dug during Roman times, and small deposits of gold are still available in the Dolgellau area in North Wales, and near Pumsaint in South Wales. Coal has been dug regularly since the 17th century, and became the main extractive industry in the 19th and 20th centuries. Iron making was booming in the 19th century, with Merthyr Tydfil in the South Wales valleys the most important center for a considerable period. Steel making is still an important industry in South Wales, with the main works at Port Talbot, although several plants have closed in Wales since the 1980s. Tinplate works and copper works were at their peak in the 19th century, especially in Swansea, which was once a world centre for copper. Copper ore was mined on the island of Anglesey, and slate quarrying became important in North Wales towards the end of the 19th century.

Although Welsh communities profited at various times from these industries, the country's wealth has generally been exported to foreign industrialists. Recently new industries, some based on electronics and involved in the production of television sets and other commodities, have been established. Several motor manufacturers have factories which produce engines, gears and other parts for cars. Once again, most of the wealth created by these industries is sent abroad, including the far east, rather than kept in Wales.

Farming, the wool trade and cattle rearing have been traditional industries. With the growth of extractive industries, and the need for exporting, the shipping industries became important, and many western coastal towns, such as Porthmadog and Cardigan became centers of ship building. Many of the old ports have become modern day marinas for small craft. Ports along the south coast, including Cardiff, Barry and Swansea, had a busy world-wide trade, and developed colourful dockland communities.

Wales is richly blessed in natural resources. It has ample water supplies. Its large coal resources which, even if extracted vigorously, could last another three hundred years. Many mineral deposits have been extraced, including silver and lead as well as iron, copper and gold. The country has ample agricultural land, although much of it is in upland areas, and is used for rearing sheep, of which some 12,000,000 are seen roaming in all parts of the country. Coal and water have been used to create electricity, of which there is ample supply through various power stations. Recently advances have been made using wind power.

The finance and service industries have been developing at a pace at the end of the twentieth century, and Cardiff, the capital city, is by now a financial and institutional centre of importance.

In spite of all these riches, Wales has constantly been a country of comparatively high unemployment in the twentieth century. The economic scene was ravaged by the depression of the 1920s and 1930s, when half a million people left the country to find work elsewhere. This led to some valley coal mining communities having unemployment rates of up to 70%. The official figures of the 1990s reveal a general unemployment rate of around 8%, but as the way of counting these figures has been changed around 20 times for cosmetic effect, the real figure must be double this amount, and in certain parts of the socially deprived industrial valleys and of rural Wales, the figure is far higher.

Nevertheless, much progress has been made in developing the economy in certain parts of Wales, especially the south-east. The Welsh Development Agency, formed in 1976 to tackle some of the worst hit areas, prides itself in attracting inward investment, but it is sometimes criticized for concentrating development in the areas nearest to the south and north roads which lead to England, rather than creating a sound infrastructure for the development of an all Wales economy.

LITERATURE AND ARTS

The first known Welsh poem was written around 600AD, and since then Wales has had an unbroken tradition of Welsh language literature. The early poets held important posts in the courts of the princes, and were regarded as educators, historians and entertainers. The important position of the poets under the old order continued after the death of the last of the Welsh princes in 1282, and they became the poets of the gentry. Welsh poetry experienced a golden age between 1300 - 1500, and its most well-known poet, Dafydd ap Gwilym, wrote joyously about love, life, religion and nature in the 14th century.

Wales is also rich in tales. Mediaeval tales were recounted orally, in a tradition linked with Ireland and other European countries. The best known tales of this period are the Mabinogi, or Mabinogion. They relate adventures associated with figures of Welsh, Irish and Roman history and with Celtic deity, and include many folk themes which are in common with the Indo-European tradition.

The translation of the Bible into Welsh in 1588 was an important development, and led to the flowering of modern literature. Hymn writing later gave way to romantic poetry, the development of the novel and plays.

One institution which has supported Welsh literature throughout the centuries is the Eisteddfod, where traditionally bards compete with each other to win one of two main prizes, the chair and the crown. The first known eisteddfod was held by Lord Rhys ap Gruffudd at Cardigan in 1176. Around 1500 the bards held several important eisteddfodau in order to keep the bardic order and to establish rules of writing poetry. These included the intricate cynghanedd (harmony) where strict rules regarding repetition of consonants and rhyme govern each line of writing. The winner of the chair in the National Eisteddfod, held for a week annually in present day Wales, must write a poem using these intricate rules.

The golden age of Welsh publishing was the 19th century, when a literate populace read avidly. A 10 volume encyclopedia, scores of magazines and newspapers and hundreds of books on all kinds of subjects were among the products of a successful publishing industry.

The twentieth century has seen another period of constantly developing writing. Among the best know writers are Gwenallt (pacifist Christian nationalist poet), Waldo Williams (pacifist nattionalist poet), Kate Roberts (novelist and short story writer on the slate quarry communities), Saunders Lewis (playwright, poet, literary critic), Islwyn Ffowc Elis (novelist), Gwyn Thomas (poet), Gerallt Lloyd Owen (nationalist poet).

Welsh language arts developed with the advent of radio and television. Welsh language radio is available all day, and the present Welsh TV channel, S4C, which has previously broadcast 3 - 4 hours of Welsh per evening is developing into an all day Welsh language channel. This has led to popular Welsh soap operas (especially *Pobl y Cwm* , the People of the Valley) and films. There are around fifty independent television companies operating in Wales, as well as around ten active publishing houses.

Welsh performers have flourished in the musical world, both in traditional opera - the Welsh National Opera Company has won world-wide acclaim - and popular entertainment. Among prominent names of the second half of the 20th century are Geraint Evans, Bryn Terfel, (opera), Shirley Bassey, Tom Jones, Harry Secombe and Mary Hopkin (singers and entertainers).

There has been a growth in interest in the twentieth century in the work of Welsh artists. Richard Wilson (18th century) belonged to the romantic school. Evans Walters (20th century) from Swansea was an impressionist painter, depicting many local people and scenes, while Augustus John and his sister Gwen Jones also developed from the impressionist era. Ceri Richards was a foremost symbolist, and Kyffin Williams (born 1918) is a powerful landscape painter.

English language writing in Wales has come into its own in the 20th century. The perceived anti-Welsh writings of Caradoc Evans (short stories) and Gwyn Thomas (stories and plays) hindered its acceptance, but Dylan Thomas' fame as a poet has continued to grow. With the nationalist vision of writers such as R.S. Thomas (poet) and other recent writers, English medium writing in Wales in now a part of Wales' literary tradition.

Welsh popular singing in Welsh and English has developed simultaneously. Dafydd Iwan is the most popular Welsh folk singer. In the pop scene recent successful groups include the bilingual Super Furry Animals and Catatonia.

FATE OF THE LANGUAGE

Around 500,000 people speak Welsh today, some 20% of the population. The future of Welsh, just as in the case of several other non-state languages in Europe, is not yet secure, although many advances have been made in the latter half of the twentieth century.

Welsh had from the 16th century lost its status as the language of law, government and administration. Nevertheless, in spite of the 1536 Act of Annexation which aimed at doing away with the language, the language flourished as the language of society and religion, especially after the translation of the Bible in 1588. Its use in popular education movements strengthened its position, and it continued to flourish until the mid 19th century in spite of its lack of official status.

A report on education in Wales in 1847 denounced the Welsh for their lack of knowledge in English, at a time when the masters of industry were largely monoglot English. This gave rise to an inferiority complex in the Welsh and a lack of confidence in their own language. Welsh children came to be punished for speaking Welsh in schools, and when after 1870 primary education was made compulsory, English became the only language of education in Wales. This was followed by mass immigration into Wales of mainly English speaking people, and by the end of the 19th century, the linguistic pattern of Wales was changing rapidly.

During the course of the 20th century, which started with 50% of the people of Wales able to speak Welsh, its position was further weakened and eroded by economic and political forces. Some 20,000 Welsh speakers were killed in the First World War, and in the following twenty years around 250,000 Welsh speakers emigrated to England and beyond during the years of economic depression. A further 6,000 Welsh speakers were killed in the Second World War.

With the advent of mass media, and the continually expanding influence of Anglo-american popular culture, and the ever-centralizing forces of London government and administration, the Welsh language continued to lose ground. English became more and more the language of work, commerce, education, and popular culture. The numbers of Welsh speakers, especially in south-east Wales, fell as Welsh was not transmitted in the homes, and the areas which had a majority of Welsh speakers declined.

By the end of the twentieth century, very few places in Wales had more than 80% Welsh speakers, although large areas of north and west Wales still have more than 50% Welsh speakers. The notion of a Wesh speaking Wales is largely attributed to west and north Wales, but this does not take into account the large numbers of Welsh speakers who live in the south. Numerically, more people speak Welsh in south than in north Wales.

To counteract the continual reduction in numbers of Welsh speakers, many Welsh people strove to set up organizations and bodies that could further the language. One of the most successful is Urdd Gobaith Cymru - the Welsh League of Youth - a youth movement established by Ifan ab Owen Edwards in 1922. This movement has attractive youth camps and organizes a hugely successful annual eisteddfod.

In 1925 the Welsh national party - Plaid Cymru - was founded, with the aim of creating a Welsh speaking, self-governing country. Although the party did not have much political success before Gwynfor Evans became Member of Parliament for Carmarthen in 1966, it has been a forceful pressure group, and has influenced the political thinking of all parties. It has also fought many successful campaigns which have seen the Welsh language gain a respectable place on radio and television, and as a language of administration.

One of the most successful movements has been the parents, individuals and bodies who have been responsible for the growth of Welsh medium and bilingual education. The first Welsh medium primary schools were established after the Second World War, and by the end of the 20th Century, around 450 primary schools in Wales were teaching through the medium of Welsh. This increase was produced to some extent by the huge popularity of Mudiad Ysgolion Meithrin - the Welsh medium playgroup movement, established in 1971, which now attracts around 15,000 children under 5 years of age to its preschool playgroups. Secondary education through the medium of Welsh has also flourished, with around 50 schools teaching some subjects through the medium of Welsh, and around 25 teaching mainly through the medium of Welsh. By the mid 1990s, Welsh became a compulsory subject in almost all English medium schools in Wales. The effect of this growth is that 25% of Welsh primary schools are now Welsh medium schools, and there has been an increase of Welsh speaking children and young people over the last twenty years. This gives sound hope for the future.

The number of adults learning Welsh has also increased annually. Courses are organized by many bodies, including the University of Wales and local colleges. Around 20,000 attend courses each year, and this number is augmented by those who learn Welsh through popular books, radio and television programmes. CYD is an organization that caters for learners of Welsh throughout the country, organizing social events locally.

Cymdeithas yr Iaith Gymraeg, the Welsh Language Society, was established in 1962 as a pressure group to ensure for Welsh a measure of official status. It adopted non-violent, civil disobedience as a form of action, and this brought swift results. A Welsh Language Act was passed in 1967, and a second Welsh Language Act in 1993. These have ensured that Welsh is used daily by all local authorities and public bodies. Bilingual road signs were the norm by the mid 1970s, and S4C, the partly Welsh television channel, was established in 1982. This movement has attracted much support from young people, and has given rise to popular Welsh music and culture.

Many other movements have supported activities in Welsh, not least the annual Welsh national eisteddfod, which lasts a week. Music, poetry, art, prose, singing and reciting competitions are held daily, with many other activities, e.g. a rock music tent, catering for many tastes. The Books Council of Wales, established in the early 1960s, promotes Welsh publishing, and many publishing houses produce between 400 and 500 Welsh language books annually. Several recording companies supply a constant stream of Welsh language music. Welsh literature and Welsh medium culture have flourished in the last thirty years.

Welsh is a thriving Celtic language. Indeed the vigour of Welsh culture and the youth of its speakers augur well for the future.

PRACTICAL ADVICE FOR EVERYDAY LIFE

Arriving
Most people travelling to Wales will probably first arrive at one of England's major airports, such as Heathrow or Gatwick or Birmingham, although some aeroplanes form New York and Canada arrive at Wales International Airport, Cardiff. The regulations regarding passport and visa are the same as for the U.K. generally.

The same regulations for tolls apply as for the U.K. and the European Union generally.

Roads and railways
The main road into southern Wales is the M4 motorway from London to South Wales, which passes near Cardiff and Swansea, and continues as a dual carriageway past Carmarthen. The main road into northern Wales along the north Wales coast is the A55 dual carriageway from Chester which leads eventually to Bangor, linking with the A5 to Holyhead, Anglesey. The A40 main road comes into Wales from the English midlands, and is a convenient road for mid Wales.

The main railway lines into Wales are again in the north and south. From London, there is an hourly service to Cardiff and Swansea from Paddington station, and the line continues to Pembrokeshire. In north Wales, the line from Chester extends, like the road, to Holyhead. Aberystwyth on the mid west Wales coast is reached by a line from Shrewbury and Birmingham. The rail network has been privatized and is split between several companies, but the ticket offices can supply you with tickets to all destinations. The price structure is complicated, with better prices available for advance bookings.

Most of the roads in Wales, apart from those mentioned, are single carriageway, and due to the hilly nature of the country, many can be winding and some are narrow, but they are generally in good condition. There is an ample number of filling stations throughout the country.

Speed limit for automobiles are similar to the U.K.:
    in urban areas: 30m.p.h.
    elsewhere: 60 m.p.h.
    motorways: 70 m.p.h.

There is a daily bus service between north and south Wales, from Cardiff, via Swansea, Carmarthen, Lampeter, Aberystwyth, Dolgellau to Bangor. By rail one must travel via Shrewsbury or Crewe from Swansea or Cardiff, although there is a train service, passing beautiful scenery, from Aberystwyth to the north.

The two main automobile associations are the A.A. and the R.A.C. which supply roadside help. Many car rental services operate, e.g. Hertz, Avis and others.

Money, shopping and services
The same money system as the U.K. applies, with 100 pence in a pound (£). Credit cards are accepted by most businesses and hotels. Banks are usually open from 9.30 to 15.30 from Monday to Friday, but many branches in towns are also open later and on Saturday mornings. Most bank branches have 24 hour cash dispensing machines. Post Offices are open from 9.00 to 17.30 from Monday to Friday, and on Saturday mornings until 12.30. Most main branches can exchange money on the spot, and this and many other services are now available at main post offices and in travel agencies.

Services
Emergency services (police, fire, ambulance): phone 999
Telephone operator: 100
Telephone enquiries: 192
Public telephones vary. Some can be used with coins (10p, 20p, 50p or £1), others with phone cards (bought at post offices and

newsagents, valued at £2, £5 and £10) or with personal credit cards. Some cater for both cards and coins.

BT is the main telephone company, and it produces telephone directories. Other telephone services are also available.

Telephone codes for some towns:

Cardiff: 01222;   Swansea: 01792; Carmarthen: 01267; Aberystwyth: 01970;   Bangor: 01248;   Caernarfon: 01286 (from abroad drop the first '0')

Code for telephoning the U.S.A.: 001

Shopping

Shops are usually open from 9.00 to 5.30 from Friday to Saturday, although some shops are also open on Sunday, from 10.00 to 16.00.

Some shops specialize in Welsh crafts, and their products include woolen materials and clothes. There are many outlets for Welsh pottery and slate products, and wooden carvings, e.g. Welsh love spoons. Recordings of Welsh choirs, including male voice choirs and 'penillion' singing - where the melody on the accompanying harp is harmonized by the singers - are popular presents, as are recordings of Welsh folk and popular music. Jewellery from Welsh gold, made by Welsh craftspeople, are also popular, as are silver and other metal jewellery, fashioned in Celtic designs.

Most towns and villages have a local sell-all shop, in the form of a corner shop or a small supermarket, while most towns have out of town shopping centeres as well as a shopping high street and indoor shopping centers.

Most towns also have a market which sells local produce, and these are always well worth a visit.

There are Welsh bookshops in most towns. These sell books, tapes and CDs and Welsh craft. Most general bookshops also sell books of Welsh interest and a smaller selection of Welsh books.

Restaurants and pubs
There are plenty of restaurants and public houses, with many serving decent food. Many are renowned for their Welsh atmosphere, while those in large towns usually tend to present a more anglicized or European environment. There are plenty of Welsh pubs in places where most people speak Welsh, in towns such as Aberystwyth, Porthmadog, Bala, Caernarfon, Carmarthen and Lampeter, in scores of villages and generally in Gwendraeth and Amman valleys. Many sport a selection of antiques and rustic utensils. Cardiff has a Welsh club (Clwb Ifor Bach) and so has Swansea (Tŷ Tawe), where Welsh is the natural language of conversation.

Restaurants often supply local foods: lamb, beef and pork are popular, as well as sea food and river fish, with locally caught lobsters, salmon, sewin and trout often among the fare. Other local delicacies include cockles and laver bread (Swansea area). There is an ample supply of Indian, Chinese and Italian restaurants in most towns. Prices vary enormously according to the class of restaurant while more and more pubs now offer bar meals and full meals, and they often offer better value than restaurants. The Welsh Tourist Board (Brunel House, Cardiff) can supply a list of good restaurants.

Public houses were closed on Sundays until about the 1980s, but following local referenda, all such establishments are now open every day of the week, from around 11.00 until around 23.00.

Tipping is only usual with full meals in restaurants, but is not necessary. Up to 10% of the bill is fairly usual.

Accommodation
There is a full range of hotels, guesthouses and private 'bed and breakfast' houses in most areas. A list of verified accommodation can be obtained from the Welsh Tourist Board or from the 22 county authorities, while the independent

wanderer should have no difficulty in finding suitable bed and breakfast accommodation. There are plenty of camp sites for tents and caravans.

Recreation and tourism
Wales offers many delights for the tourist. As a hilly and mainly rural country, it offers ample opportunities for walking, hill walking, climbing and camping. Most towns have a public swimming pool, and many private and public golf courses are available to all at comparatively cheap rates. Public parks have facilities for tennis and other sports.

The Welsh scenery abounds in mountains and lakes, and the large coastline offers beautiful beaches and spectacular rocks, particularly in Pembrokeshire, Gower and the Llŷn peninsula. Snowdonia attracts several million tourists annually. Snowdon is the most popular mountain, and it has several well marked paths and a train ride to the summit, but those looking for a more solitary experience should wander the surrounding mountains.

The natural lakes, such as Llyn Tegid (Bala Lake) provide wonderful scenery and opportunities for water activities, and these have been augmented by the man made reservoirs, such as Clywedog, Nant y Moch and Vyrnwy in mid Wales, many of which drowned Welsh villages to supply water to England, much to the consternation of Welsh people.

The country is full of historic sites. Castles, ruined abbeys, standing stones and dolmens abound, spanning many thousands of years of history. Sense of time is intense. Most of the castles, many of which were built by the Normans in the 12th, 13th and 14th centuries (e.g. Caernarfon, Conwy, Harlech, Caerphilly), are now in a fair state of repair, and can be visited. Some castles built by the Welsh princes, such as Dinefwr, near Llandeilo, Dolbadarn and Dolwyddelan in north Wales, can also be visited. The abbeys were largely destroyed with the advent of

Protestanism in the 16th century, but those at Tintern, Valle Crucis, Neath, and other places offer strongly romantic visual images of a rich past. Dolmens, such as Pentre Ifan in Pembrokeshire and Barclodiad y Gawres (the giant's apron) in Anglesey, offer a glimpse of stone age rituals of around 2,000 B.C.

Sporting attractions include rugby and football games from autumn to early summer, and cricket, athletics and tennis in summer.

Tourist attractions include fair grounds, leisure parks, country parks, museums, castles and caves. Among the most popular are the Country Park, Llanberis (near the foot of Snowdon), the Welsh Folk Museum at St. Fagans, near Cardiff, the Llechwedd slate caverns at Blaenau Ffestiniog and Caernarfon Castle. Wales National Museum at Cardiff, Conway castle, Cardiff castle and the Brecon Beacons, the highest mountain range in southern Wales, are other major attractions.

Further travelling to Ireland is possible from Fishguard, Pembroke and Swansea in south Wales and from Holyhead in the north.

Meeting people
Welsh people are warm hearted and humorous, so little formality is needed, even in fairly formal situations. Shake hands on meeting for the first time, but not after this. People will always ask you from where you come, and to whom you may be related, or what personal or local connections you may have, so be eloquent on this. Less important is the work you do.

Some social manners take some time to get used to. If you offer a drink, a Welshman may at first say no in order to be polite. This may be repeated a second time. On the third offer he/she will probably accept. This seems to be in keeping with the addage 'three tries for a Welshman'. If a Welshman asks a guest if he wants a drink, it usually is a sign that he himself wants one, so don't refuse without making a similar offer.

In pubs, it is usual for one of the guests to buy a drink for all friends, if the number is not too great. This favor is then returned, with each guest buying a round in turn.

If you are invited to a Welsh home, don't arrive early, but try to arrive within fifteen minutes. Any gifts you bring, such as small momentos or a bottle of wine, would be most gratefully received.

National holidays

New year's day	1 January
Good Friday	The Friday before Easter Day
Easter Monday	The Monday following Easter Day
May Day	The first Monday in May
Spring Holiday	The last Monday in May
Summer Holiday	The last Monday in August
Christmas Day	25 December
Boxing Day	26 December
National Saint's Day	1 March (but is not a public holiday)

THE WELSH LANGUAGE

The Welsh language belongs to the Celtic group of languages which has two branches with Gaelic, Irish and Manx on one side and Welsh, Breton and Cornish on the other. It derives from the Indo-European family of languages, along with Germanic, Romance and many other linguistic groups.

Dialects in Wales today vary according to accent, vocabulary and construction, although all dialects can be understood by most Welsh speakers. The dialects can be broadly split into north Walian and south Walian groups, although this is an over-simplification, as geographic remoteness, caused by mountain ranges, has given rise to many local characteristics.

Standard literary Welsh, boosted by the popular preaching in nonconformist chapels in the 19th and 20th centuries, is used as the language of broadcasting, public administration and higher education today. Attempts have been made in recent years to establish a Welsh grammar more akin to the spoken language, although the main elements of vocabulary and syntax are the same. This book follows broadly this more recent grammar.

The one sound in Welsh that is not used in English is the voiceless 'll', pronounced by blowing voicelessly with the tongue and lips in the 'l' position.

Welsh Grammar

The verb forms and grammar used in this book are referred to here, with the lessons where they are introduced:

Present tense: lesson 1, 2, 3, 4, 5, 6, 7

Bod ('to be') and all verbs linked to it:

> (to introduce verbs, use ''n' or 'yn' after these forms)

present tense:

rwy/ rydw i / wi	I am
rwyt ti	you are
mae e	he / it is
mae hi	she / it is
mae Huw	Huw is
mae'r plant	the children are
rydyn ni /ry'n ni	we are
rydych chi /ry'ch chi	you are
maen nhw	they are

question forms:

ydw i?	am I?
wyt ti?	are you?
ydy e?	is he /it?
ydy hi?	is she / it?
ydy Huw?	is Huw?
ydy'r plant?	are the children?
ydyn ni?	are we?
ydych chi?	are you?
ydyn nhw?	are they?

negative forms:

dw i ddim	I am not
dwyt ti ddim	you are not
dyw e ddim	he / it is not
dyw hi ddim	she / it is not
dyw Huw ddim	Huw is not
dyw'r plant ddim	the children are not
dy'n ni ddim	we are not
dy'ch chi ddim	you are not
dy'n nhw ddim	they are not

Future: lesson 2
future tense:

bydd hi	it will be

question form:

fydd hi?	will it be?

negative form:

fydd hi ddim	it will not be

Past tense (perfect): lesson 10
perfect tense:

rwy /rydw i /wi wedi	I have
rwyt ti wedi	you have
mae e wedi	he has
etc.	

question forms:

ydw i wedi?	have I?
wyt ti wedi?	have you?
etc.	

negative forms:

dw i ddim wedi	I have not
dwyt ti ddim wedi	you have not
etc.	

Past tense (imperfect): lesson 13
imperfect tense:

roeddwn i / ro'n i	I was
roeddet ti / ro't ti	you were
roedd e	he / it was
roedd hi	he / it was
roedd Huw	Huw was
roedd y plant	the children were
roedden ni / ro'n ni	we were
roeddech chi / ro'ch chi	you were
roedden nhw / ro'n nhw	they were

question forms:

o'n i?	Was I?
o't ti?	were you?
oedd e?	was he / it?
oedd hi?	was she / it?
oedd Huw?	was Huw?
oedd y plant?	were the children?
o'n ni?	were we?
o'ch chi?	were you?
o'n nhw?	were they?

negative forms:

do'n i ddim	I wasn't
do't ti ddim	you weren't
doedd e ddim	he / it wasn't
doedd hi ddim	she / it wasn't
doedd Huw ddim	Huw wasn't
doedd y plant ddim	the children weren't
do'n ni ddim	we weren't
do'ch chi ddim	you weren't
do'n nhw ddim	they weren't

Pluperfect: lesson 13

ro'n i wedi	I had
ro't ti wedi	you had
roedd e wedi	he / it had
etc	

question forms:

o'n i wedi?	had I?
o't ti wedi?	had you?
oedd e wedi?	had he / it?
etc.	

Verb: commands: lesson 14

Add '-wch' to the stem of the verb

e.g.   cysgu: to sleep

cysgwch!	go to sleep

Verbs: past tense, short form: lesson 16

Add these endings to the stem of the verb
e.g. codi: to get up

cod**es** i	I got up
cod**est** ti	you got up
cod**odd** e	he got up
cod**odd** hi	she got up
cod**odd** Huw	Huw got up
cod**odd** y plant	the children got up
cod**on** ni	we got up
cod**och** chi	you got up
cod**on** nhw	they got up

Numbers: lesson 3

1 un	6 chwe(ch)
2 dau	7 saith
3 tri	8 wyth
4 pedwar	9 naw
5 pum (p)	10 deg

Numbers are usually followed by a singular noun

Gender of words: lesson 8

All Welsh nouns are either masculine or feminine.
Some can be both. The main differences in use are (i) feminine nouns are soft mutated after the definite article (the) 'y'; (ii) adjectives following feminine nouns are soft mutated.

Adjectives: lesson 9

Most adjectives in Welsh follow the noun. Adjectives following feminine nouns soft mutate.

e.g.	bachgen bach	small boy
	merch fach	small girl

Mutations: lesson 8, 14

These changes can occur to the initial letters of words:
Soft mutation:

c > g	p > b	t > d
g > /	b > f	d > dd
ll > l	m > f	rh > r

Aspirate mutation:

c > ch	p > ph	t > th

Nasal mutation:

c > ngh	p > mh	t > nh
g > ng	b > m	d > n

Plurals: lesson 11

There are many ways of forming plurals to Welsh nouns. The most common is adding '-au' to the noun.

Phrases using prepositions: lesson 12

Most common prepositions:

i	to	am	for
ar	on	at	to
gan	by	heb	without
o	of, from	dan	under
dros	over	drwy	through
wrth	by	yn	in

Possessive pronouns: lesson 14

fy ... i	my	ein ... ni	our
dy ... di	your	eich ... chi	your
ei ... e	his	eu ... nhw	their
ei ... hi	her		

Possessive pronouns as object of verbs: lesson 15

These possessive pronouns, when put around verbs, become the object of the verb. Note the mutations which occur with these.

e.g.	talu	*to pay*
	fy nhalu i	to pay me
	dy dalu di	to pay you
	ei dalu e	to pay him
	ei thalu hi	to pay her
	ein talu ni	to pay us
	eich talu chi	to pay you
	eu talu nhw	to pay them

Noun clauses: lesson 15

'that' is translated by 'bod'
The possessive prounouns, put around 'bod', are used to express pronouns:

fy mod i	that I am
dy fod di	that you are
ei fod e	that he is
ei bod hi	that she is
bod Huw	that Huw is
bod y plant	that the children are
ein bod ni	that we are
eich bod chi	that you are
eu bod nhw	that they are

Passive use of verbs: lesson 17

'to be' (paid) is translated by 'cael'
The possessive pronoun is put around cael:

talu	*to pay*
rwy'n cael fy nhalu	I'm being paid
rwyt ti'n cael dy dalu	you're being paid
mae e'n cael ei dalu	he's being paid
mae hi'n cael ei thalu	she's being paid
mae Huw'n cael ei dalu	Huw's being paid
mae'r plant yn cael eu talu	the children are being paid
ry'n ni'n cael ein talu	we're being paid
ry'ch chi'n cael eich talu	you're being paid
maen nhw'n cael eu talu	they're being paid

LANGUAGE
LESSONS

PRONUNCIATION GUIDE

Welsh is a fairly phonetic language: most letters have just one sound, while others vary comparatively little. A main difference to English is that it has seven vowel letters (a, e, i, o, u, w, y). Another is that it has eight combination letters which stand for one sound (ch, dd, ff, ng, ll, ph, rh, th).

The accent on almost all Welsh words is on the last syllable but one. The few exceptions include words which have an 'h' before the last syllable (e.g. mwyn**hau** - enjoy) and where the accent is noted by ^ or ˋ, (e.g. cania**tâd** - permission).

THE WELSH ALPHABET
CONSONANTS

	English equivalent	Example	Pronunciation	Meaning
b	b	baban	bahban	baby
c	k	ci	kee	dog
ch	ch (as in 'lo**ch**')	chwech	chooehch	six
d	d	dyn	deen	man
dd	th (voiced, as in **that**)	dydd	deeth	day
f	v	fi	vee	me
ff	ff (as in o**ff**)	fferm	ffehrm	farm
g	g (hard as in **game**)	gardd	gahrth	garden
ng	usually ng (as in wi**ng**)	angladd	ahnglath	funeral
	n-g (as in a**ng**ry)	Bangor	Ban-gor	Bangor
h	h	haul	haheel	sun
j	j	jam	jam	jam
l	l	lôn	loan	lane
ll	ll (position mouth for 'l' and blow voicelessly)	lle	lleh	place
m	m	mam	mam	mother

n	n	ni	nee	we
p	p	plant	plant	children
ph	ff	traphont	traffont	viaduct
r	r (trilled)	radio	rahdyo	radio
rh	rh (trilled with h)	rhaff	rhahff	spade
s	s (as in soon)	seren	sehrehn	star
t	t	tŷ	tee	house
th	th (voiceless, as in **th**ing)	cath	kahth	cat

VOWELS

	English equivalent	Example	Pronunciation	Meaning
a	a (short, as in Americ**a**	dant	dant	tooth
	ah (long, as in p**ar**k)	tân	tahn	fire
e	e (short, as in w**e**nt)	pert	pert	pretty
	eh (long, as in caf**é**)	peth	pehth	thing
	ee (after 'a' and 'o', as in w**ee**k)	mae oes?	mahee ohees	there is is there?
i	i (short, as in p**i**n)	pin	pin	pin
	ee (long, as in w**ee**k)	sgrîn	sgreen	screen
o	o (short, as in g**o**ne)	ton	ton	wave
	oa (long, as in f**o**re)	côr	coar	choir
u	i (short, as in p**i**n)	gwefus	gooehvis	lip
	ee (long, as in w**ee**k)	un	een	one
	French 'u' (in north Wales only)	pur	'pur'	pure

w	oo	hwn	hoon	this
	(short as in p**u**ll)			
	oo	cŵn	koon	dogs
	(long, as in f**oo**l)			
y	i	hyn	hin	these
	(short, as in p**i**n)			
	uh	gyrru	guhree	to drive
	(as in f**u**n)			
	ee	dyn	deen	man
	(long, as in w**ee**k)			
	(In north Wales this 'y' is pronounced like the French 'u')			

Other combinations:

si	sh	siop	shop	shop
wy	ooee	wy	ooee	egg
sh	sh	brwsh	broosh	brush

Some words sound similar to English and mean the same:

Welsh	English	Welsh	English
bag	bag	lifft	lift
banc	bank	lili	lilly
beic	bike	map	map
camera	camera	marmalêd	marmalade
casét	cassette	mat	mat
cês	case	nonsens	nonsense
cic	kick	pac	pack
cloc	clock	pas	pass
desg	desk	pinc	pink
eliffant	elephant	pot	pot
fforc	fork	problem	problem
ffresh	fresh	record	record
gêm	game	sgrîn	screen
golff	golf	sinema	cinema
inc	ink	tic	tick
jam	jam	tun	tin
jîns	jeans	winc	wink
lamp	lamp		

Some words sound fairly similar to English and mean the same:

Welsh	pronunciation	English
basged	bahsged	basket
bws	boos	bus
carped	kahrped	carpet
palas	pahlahs	palace
papur	pahpir	paper
peint	peheent	pint
radio	rahdyo	radio
stryd	streed	street
traffig	traffig	traffic
trên	trehn	train
theatr	thehatr	theater

Some words sound similar to English but have a different meaning

Welsh	pronunciation	meaning
crap	crap	smattering
cul	keel	narrow
dim	dim	nothing
dyn	Dean	man
ffrog	frog	frock
haws	house	easier
hi	he	she
hy	he	bold
hynt	hint	journey
lôn	loan	lane
mil	meal	thousand
min	mean	edge
pump	pimp	five
tri	tree	three
tyn	tin	tight

Some personal names are pronounced similarly:

Welsh	English
Beti	Betty
Efa	Eva
Ffransis	Francis
Gruffudd	Griffith
Henri	Henry
Huw	Hugh
Rhys	Rees

Pronunciation of place names and their English equivalent:

Welsh	pronunciation	English
Abertawe	Ahbehrtahooeh	Swansea
Aberteifi	Ahbehrteheevee	Cardigan
Caerdydd	Kaheer-deeth	Cardiff
Caerfyrddin	Kaheervuhrddin	Carmarthen
Cei Newydd	Kehee Nehooith	New Quay
Cydweli	Kidwehlee	Kidwelly
Dinbych	Dinbich	Denbigh
Hwlffordd	Hoolffordd	Haverfordwest
Môn	Moan	Anglesey
Pen y Bont	Pen uh Bont	Bridgend
Talacharn	Talahcharn	Laugharne
Tŷ Ddewi	Tee Thehooee	St. David's
Trallwng	Tralloong	Welshpool

GWERS UN: CWRDD
LESSON ONE: MEETING

Helo	Hello
Shwmae	Hello (South Wales)
Sut 'dach chi	How are you (North Wales)
Shwd ych chi	How are you (South Wales)
Falch i gwrdd â chi	Pleased to meet you
Yn dda iawn	Very well
Bore da	Good morning
Prynhawn da	Good afternoon
Noswaith dda	Good evening
Nos da	Good night
Ydych chi'n siarad.....?	Do you speak .... ?
Ydw	Yes (I do)
Rwy'n deall Cymraeg	I understand Welsh
Na	No
Hwyl!	Good-bye
Pob hwyl!	Good-bye

GRAMADEG: GRAMMAR

Ydych	chi	'n	siarad	Cymraeg?
Do	*you*		*speak*	*Welsh?*

The **'n** following **chi** introduces the verb **siarad** (*speak*). It has no meaning of its own, except for continuing the tense (time) of the original verb **ydych** (*do*).

The above table can be extended to include more languages:

Ydych chi'n siarad	Cymraeg (*Welsh*)?
	Saesneg (*English*)?
Do you speak	Ffrangeg (*French*)?
	Almaeneg (*German*)?
	Sbaeneg (*Spanish*)?
	Eidaleg (*Italian*)?

Ydw - *yes* (*I do*)
Na - *no*

To say '*I speak*' use 'Rwy' or 'Rydw i' instead of 'Ydych':

Rwy		'n	siarad	Cymraeg
Rydw	i	'n		
or	*I talk Welsh* *I am talking Welsh*			

This can be extended to include other verbs and to include more languages:

Rwy		'n	siarad	Cymraeg
Rydw	i		deall	Ffrangeg
				Almaeneg
				Sbaeneg
				Eidaleg

speak *talk*
deall *understand*

47

Huw:	Shwmae!
Janet:	Helo! Bore da!
Huw:	Bore da! Shwd ych chi?
Janet:	Yn dda iawn. Shwd ych chi?
Huw:	Yn dda iawn. Ydych chi'n deall Cymraeg?
Janet:	Ydw, tipyn bach. Ydych chi'n siarad Cymraeg?
Huw:	Ydw, rwy'n siarad Cymraeg. Ydych chi'n siarad Cymraeg?
Janet:	Ydw, tipyn bach.
Huw:	Falch i gwrdd â chi.
Janet:	Falch i gwrdd â chi hefyd.

Alun:	Noswaith dda!
Sian:	Noswaith dda!
Alun:	Aha! Ydych chi'n siarad Cymraeg?
Sian:	Ydw, tipyn bach. Ond siaradwch yn araf.
Alun:	Sut 'dach chi?
Sian:	Beth?
Alun:	Sut 'dach chi? - Shwd ych chi?
Sian:	O! Shwd ych chi! Yn dda iawn diolch. A shwd ych chi?
Alun:	Rwy'n dda iawn, diolch!
Sian:	Hwyl!
Alun:	Pob hwyl!

Huw:	Hello!
Janet:	Hello! Good morning!
Huw:	Good morning! How are you?
Janet:	Very well. How are you?
Huw:	Very well. Do you understand Welsh?
Janet:	Yes, a little. Do you speak Welsh?
Huw:	Yes, I speak Welsh. Do you speak Welsh?
Janet:	Yes, a little.
Huw:	Pleased to meet you.
Janet:	Pleased to meet you too.

Alun:	Good evening!
Sian:	Good evening!
Alun:	Aha! Do you speak Welsh?
Sian:	Yes, a little. But speak slowly.
Alun:	How are you?
Sian:	What?
Alun:	How are you? - How are you?
Sian:	Oh! How are you! Very well, thanks. And how are you?
Alun:	I'm very well, thanks.
Sian:	Good-bye!
Alun:	Good-bye!

GEIRFA: VOCABULARY

deall	-	(to) understand
tipyn bach	-	a little
cwrdd	-	(to) meet
diolch	-	thanks
a	-	and
siaradwch	-	talk
yn araf	-	slowly
beth	-	what

YMARFERION: EXCERCISES

1. Read the Welsh aloud, several times. Practice with a friend if possible.

2. Cover the English side. Translate the Welsh. Check after each sentence, then attempt it all. Do this several times.

3. Cover the Welsh side. Translate the English. Check after each sentence, then attempt it all. Do this several times.

4. Make up as many questions as you can, selecting words from each column:

Ydych	chi'n deall	siarad	Cymraeg? Ffrangeg? Saesneg? Eidaleg? Sbaeneg? Almaeneg?

5. Answer the questions you have made, by choosing the appropriate answer from this list:

      Ydw, rwy'n gallu siarad Cymraeg
      Ydw, tipyn bach
      Na
      Ydw, rwy'n deall Eidaleg

6. Say which languages you speak or understand, e.g.

      Rwy'n siarad Almaeneg
      Rwy'n deall Ffrangeg

Rwy'n	deall siarad	Ffrangeg Almaeneg Saesneg Eidaleg Sbaeneg Cymraeg

EXTRA GRAMMAR

1. *What is* _____ *in Welsh?*

    Beth yw _____ yn Gymraeg?

    e.g. Beth yw 'sausage' yn Gymraeg?
          Beth yw 'Wales' yn Gymraeg?

2. | *I* | *don't* | *understand* | *Welsh.* |
    |---|---|---|---|
    | Dw i | ddim | yn deall | Cymraeg. |

I	*don't*	*speak*	*Welsh.*
Dw i	ddim	yn siarad	Cymraeg.

GWERS DAU: Y TYWYDD
LESSON TWO: THE WEATHER

mae hi'n	it is	sych	dry
bydd hi'n	it will be	heulog	sunny
bwrw glaw	raining	bwrw eira	snowing
braf	fine	dwym	warm
oer	cold	gymylog	cloudy

GRAMADEG: GRAMMAR

Form of verb 'be'	Subject	'n	verb or adjective
Mae	hi	'n	bwrw glaw
It is raining			
Mae	hi	'n	bwrw eira
It is snowing			
Mae	hi	'n	braf
It is fine			

Question and answer:

Ydy hi'n bwrw glaw?   Ydy
Is it raining?   *Yes*
Ydy hi'n sych?   Na
Is it dry?   *No*

Future:

Bydd	hi	'n	bwrw glaw
It will be raining			
Bydd	hi	'n	sych
It will be dry			

Question and answer:

Fydd hi'n braf yfory?   Bydd
Will it be fine tomorrow?   *Yes*
Fydd hi'n bwrw glaw yfory?   Na
Will it rain tomorrow?   *No*

Sian:	Bore da!
Huw:	Bore da! Mae hi'n braf.
Sian:	Ydy, mae hi'n braf iawn.
Huw:	Mae hi'n heulog heddiw.
Sian:	Mae hi'n heulog iawn.
Huw:	Mae hi'n bwrw glaw yn Aberystwyth.
Sian:	Ond mae hi'n braf yn Abertawe.

Alun:	Noswaith dda, Mari.
Mari:	Noswaith dda, Alun. Shwd ych chi?
Alun:	Yn dda iawn. Fydd hi'n braf heno?
Mari:	Bydd, bydd hi'n braf iawn.
Alun:	Fydd hi'n braf yfory?
Mari:	Na, bydd hi'n bwrw glaw.
Alun:	O daro!

Radio:	Bydd hi'n sych heno.
	Bydd hi'n bwrw glaw yn y bore.
	Bydd hi'n braf yn y prynhawn.
	Bydd hi'n oer yn y nos.

Sian:	Good morning!
Huw:	Good morning! It's fine.
Sian:	Yes, it's very fine.
Huw:	It's sunny today.
Sian:	It's very sunny.
Huw:	It's raining in Aberystwyth.
Sian:	But it's fine in Swansea.

Alun:	Good evening, Mari.
Mari:	Good evening, Alun. How are you?
Alun:	Very well. Will it be fine tonight?
Mari:	Yes, it will be very fine.
Alun:	Will it be fine tomorrow?
Mari:	No, it will rain .
Alun:	O dear!

Radio:	It will be dry tonight.
	It will rain in the morning.
	It will be fine in the afternoon.
	It will be cold in the night.

GEIRFA: VOCABULARY

iawn	very
heddiw	today
yn	in
heno	tonight
yfory	tomorrow
daro!	dear!
y nos	the night
bore ma	this morning

YMARFERION: EXCERCISES

1. Read the Welsh aloud, several times. Practice with a friend if possible.

2. Cover the English side. Translate the Welsh. Check after each sentence, then attempt it all. Do this several times.

3. Cover the Welsh side. Translate the English. Check after each sentence, then attempt it all. Do this several times.

4. Make up as many sentences as you can, selecting words from each column:

Mae	hi'n	bwrw glaw	heno
Bydd		sych	heddiw
		braf	yfory
		oer	yn y nos
		bwrw eira	yn y bore
			yn y prynhawn
			bore ma

5. Ask questions on the weather, using
Ydy hi'n ....?

or   Fydd hi'n ....?

e.g. Ydy hi'n bwrw glaw heddiw?
Ydy.
Fydd hi'n sych yfory?
Bydd

EXTRA GRAMMAR

1.   Note that 'it' is translated by 'hi' (*she*) when the weather is discussed. In other instances, 'it' is translated by 'hi' (*she*) when referring to feminine nouns, and by 'e' (*he*) when referring to masculine nouns.

2.   Saying 'it isn't':

Negative verb	subject	not	'yn'	verb
Dyw	hi	ddim	yn	bwrw glaw

It is not raining.

Dyw hi ddim yn sych   *It isn't dry*

Dyw hi ddim yn heulog   *It isn't sunny*

Dyw hi ddim yn oer   *It isn't cold*

GWERS TRI: **YN YR ORSAF**
LESSON THREE: **AT THE STATION**

pryd?	when?	un ffordd	one way
sut?	how?	dychwel	return
ble?	where?	mynd	(to) go
beth?	what?	dod	(to) come
'r	the	aros	(to) stay, (to) stop
ga i	may I have	gadael	(to) leave
tocyn	ticket	cyrraedd	(to) arrive (at)
un tocyn	one ticket	newid	change
dau docyn	two tickets	prynu	(to) buy
tri thocyn	three tickets	rhaid	must
trên	train	punt	pound
bws	bus		
tacsi	taxi		
awyren	plane		

GRAMADEG: GRAMMAR

Forming questions:

Question word	form of verb 'to be'	subject	yn *or* 'n	verb
Pryd	mae	'r trên	yn	mynd?
When is the train going?				
Ble	mae'r	bws	yn	aros?
Where does the bus stop?				
Sut	mae	Sian	yn	dod?
How is Sian coming?				
Ble	mae	'r orsaf?		
Where is the station?				
Pryd	mae	'r bws	yn	gadael?
When does the bus leave?				

Mae Janet yn cyrraedd Bangor. Mae hi yn yr orsaf. Mae hi yn y swyddfa docynnau.

Janet:	Pryd mae'r trên yn mynd i Abertawe?
Mr Evans:	Mae'r trên yn mynd i Abertawe am saith o'r gloch.
Janet:	O da iawn. Pryd mae'r trên yn cyrraedd Abertawe?
Mr Evans:	Mae e'n cyrraedd Abertawe am saith o'r gloch y nos.
Janet:	O wel, ga i un tocyn i Abertawe.
Mr Evans:	Dychwel?
Janet:	Na, un ffordd.
Mr Evans:	Tri deg punt.
Janet:	O ble mae'r trên yn mynd?
Mr Evans:	Mae'r trên yn mynd o blatfform tri.

Mae Sian yn yr orsaf bysiau yn Aberystwyth.

Sian:	Pryd mae'r bws yn mynd i Abertawe?
Mr Davies:	Mae'r bws yn mynd i Abertawe am un o'r gloch.
Sian:	Pryd mae e'n cyrraedd?
Mr Davies:	Mae e'n cyrraedd am bedwar o'r gloch.
Sian:	Dau docyn i Abertawe, os gwelwch yn dda.
Mr Davies:	Dychwel?
Sian:	Na, un ffordd.
Mr Davies:	Un deg wyth punt.
Sian:	Ble mae'r bws?
Mr Davies:	Mae'r bws fan hyn.

Janet arrives at Bangor. She is at the station. She is in the booking office (tickets office).

Janet: When does the train go to Swansea?
Mr Evans: The train goes to Swansea at seven o'clock.
Janet.   Oh very good. When does the train arrive at Swansea?
Mr Evans: The train arrives at Swansea at seven o'clock at night.
Janet: Oh well, may I have one ticket to Swansea.
Mr Evans: Return?
Janet: No, one way.
Mr Evans: Thirty pounds
Janet: From where does the train go?
Mr Evans: The train goes from platform three.

Sian is in the bus station at Aberystwyth.

Sian: When does the bus go to Swansea?
Mr Davies: The bus goes to Swansea at one o'clock.
Sian: When does it arrive?
Mr Davies: It arrives at four o'clock.
Sian: Two tickets to Swansea, please.
Mr Davies: Return?
Sian: No, one way.
Mr Davies: Eighteen pounds.
Sian: Where is the bus?
Mr Davies: The bus is here.

GEIRFA: VOCABULARY

am	at
o'r gloch	o'clock
wedyn	then
platfform	platform
fan hyn	here

NUMBERS

1 un	11 un deg un (un ar ddeg)	21 dau ddeg un
2 dau	12 un deg dau (deuddeg)	22 dau ddeg dau
3 tri	13 un deg tri	23 dau ddeg tri
4 pedwar	14 un deg pedwar	24 dau ddeg pedwar
5 pump	15 un deg pump (pymtheg)	25 dau ddeg pump
6 chwech	16 un deg chwech	26 dau ddeg chwech
7 saith	17 un deg saith	27 dau ddeg saith
8 wyth	18 un deg wyth (deunaw)	28 dau ddeg wyth
9 naw	19 un deg naw	29 dau ddeg naw
10 deg	20 dau ddeg (ugain)	30 tri deg

31 tri deg un	70 saith deg	300 tri chant
40 pedwar deg	71 saith deg un	400 pedwar cant
41 pedwar deg un	80 wyth deg	500 pum cant
50 pum deg	81 wyth deg un	600 chwe chant
51 pum deg un	90 naw deg	700 saith cant
60 chwe deg	91 naw deg un	800 wyth cant
61 chwe deg un	100 cant	900 naw cant
	200 dau gant	1000 mil

Numbers in brackets are used with time.
Numbers are usually followed by singular nouns:

£5	pum punt
£30	tri deg punt

YMARFERION: EXCERCISES

1. Read the Welsh aloud, several times.
2. Cover the English side. Translate the Welsh. Check after each sentence, then attempt it all. Do this several times.
3. Cover the Welsh side. Translate the English. Check after each sentence, then attempt it all. Do this several times.
4. Make up as many questions as you can, selecting words from each column:

Pryd	mae'r	trên	yn mynd?
		bws	yn gadael?
			yn cyrraedd?

5. Give the answers in Welsh:
   a) Pryd mae'r trên ym mynd i Aberystwyth - 8 o'clock
      e.g. Mae'r trên yn mynd i Aberystwyth am wyth o'r gloch.
   b) Pryd mae'r trên yn gadael Bangor? - 7 o'clock
   c) Pryd mae'r bws yn gadael Caerdydd? - 1 o'clock
   d) Pryd mae'r bws yn gadael Llanelli? - 6 o'clock
   e) Pryd mae'r trên yn mynd i Abertawe? - 9 o'clock

GWERS PEDWAR: CYFLWYNO
LESSON FOUR: INTRODUCTIONS

Diolch	Thanks
Diolch yn fawr	Thank you very much
Os gwelwch yn dda	Please
Huw ydw i	I am Huw
Dyma Sian	Here is Sian
Ydych chi'n nabod Sian?	Do you know Sian?
Clerc ydw i	I am a clerk
Ble ry'ch chi'n byw?	Where do you live?
Rwy'n byw yn Abertawe	I live in Swansea

GRAMADEG: GRAMMAR

Word order of Welsh sentences, present tense:

Form of verb 'to be'	Subject	yn (or 'n)	verb	object
Rydw	i	'n	hoffi	ffilmiau
I like films				
Rwyt	ti	'n	hoffi	theatr
You like theater				
Mae	e	'n	hoffi	Abertawe
He likes Swansea				
Mae	hi	'n	hoffi	Vermont
She likes Vermont				
Mae	Sian	yn	hoffi	byw yma
Sian likes living here				
Mae'r	plant	yn	hoffi	chwarae
The children like to play				
Rydyn	ni	'n	hoffi	nofio
We like to swim				
Rydych	chi	'n	hoffi	mynd
We like to go				
Maen	nhw	'n	hoffi	dod
They like to come				

Alternative forms, often heard *(pronunciations in italics)*:

Rydw i'n:	Rwy'n	Dw i'n	Wi'n
ruhdoo een	*rooeen*	*doo een*	*ooeen*
Rydyn ni'n:	Ry'n ni'n		
ruhdin neen	*reen neen*		
Rydych chi'n:	Ry'ch chi'n		
ruhdich cheen	*reech cheen*		

Mae Janet yn dod o Poultney, Vermont. Mae hi'n awr yn Abertawe.
Mae hi ar wyliau. Mae hi'n mynd i'r Clwb Cymraeg yn Abertawe.

Mair: Noswaith dda. Shwd ych chi heno?
Janet: Noswaith dda! Yn dda iawn, diolch. A chi?
Mair: Yn dda iawn. Ydych chi'n dod o Abertawe?
Janet: Na! Janet Evans ydw i. Rwy'n dod o America.
Mair: O America?
Janet: Ie. Rwy'n dod o Poultney, Vermont.
Mair: Beth ydych chi'n gwneud yn Abertawe?
Janet: Wel, rydw i yma ar wyliau: rydw i'n moyn dysgu
          Cymraeg.
Mair: Croeso i Abertawe! Falch i gwrdd â chi!
Janet: Ydych chi'n byw yn Abertawe?
Mair: Ydw. Mair Evans ydw i. Rwy'n byw yma ers pum
          mlynedd.
Janet: Ydych chi'n gweithio yma?
Mair: Ydw. Llyfrgellydd ydw i. Rwy'n gweithio yn y llyfrgell
          yn Abertawe. A chi? Ydych chi'n gweithio?
Janet: Ydw. Nyrs ydw i. Rydw i'n gweithio yn yr ysbyty yn
          Fairhaven. Rwy'n hoffi'r gwaith.
Mair: Ydych chi'n dod o Vermont?
Janet: Na, rwy'n dod o Kentucky. Ond mae Mam yn dod o
          Gymru - mae hi'n dod o Abertawe.
Mair: O ble yn Abertawe?
Janet: O'r Mwmbwls. Mae hi'n byw yn America ers hanner
          can mlynedd, ond mae hi'n hoffi dod i Abertawe ar
          wyliau.
Mair: Ydych chi'n nabod rhywun yn Abertawe?
Janet: Na, ond rydw i'n mynd i chwilio am achau'r teulu yn
          y llyfrgell. Ac rydw i'n mynd i weld popeth! Rydw i'n
          hoffi nofio, felly rydw i'n mynd i nofio yn y môr bob
          dydd. Rydw i'n hoffi'r theatr, ac rydw i'n hoffi gweld
          ffilmiau.
Mair: Dewch i'r llyfrgell gyda fi yfory!

Janet comes from Poultney, Vermont. She is now in Swansea. She is on holiday. She goes to the Welsh Club in Swansea.

Mair:	Good evening. How are you tonight?
Janet:	Good evening. Very well, thanks. And you?
Mair:	Very well. Do you come from Swansea?
Janet:	No! I'm Janet Evans. I come from America.
Mair:	From America?
Janet:	Yes. I come from Poultney, Vermont.
Mair:	What are you doing in Swansea?
Janet:	Well, I am here on holiday: I want to learn Welsh.
Mair:	Welcome to Swansea! Glad to meet you!
Janet:	Do you live in Swansea?
Mair:	Yes. I'm Mair Jones. I've lived here for five years.
Janet:	Do you work here?
Mair:	Yes. I am a librarian. I work in the library in Swansea. And you? Do you work?
Janet:	Yes. I am a nurse. I work in the hospital in Fairhaven. I like the work.
Mair:	Do you come from Vermont?
Janet:	No, I come from Kentucky. But Mom comes from Wales - she comes from Swansea.
Mair:	From where in Swansea?
Janet:	From the Mumbles. She has lived in America for fifty years, but she likes to come to Swansea on holiday.
Mair:	Do you know anyone in Swansea?
Janet:	No, but I'm going to search for the family tree in the library. And I'm going to see everything. I like swimming, so I'm going to swim in the sea each day. I like the theater, and I like to see films.
Mair:	Come to the library with me tomorrow!

GEIRFA: VOCABULARY

noswaith	evening	llyfrgellydd	librarian
dda	good	llyfrgell	library
[Adjectives follow the noun]		a / ac	and
heno	tonight	['ac' before vowels]	
dod	(to) come	nyrs	nurse
na	no	ysbyty	hospital
ie	yes	hoffi	(to) like
o	from	Mam	Mom
beth	what	ble	where
gwneud	(to) do,	hanner can	half a hundred,
	(to) make		fifty
yma	here	mynd	(to) go
ar wyliau	on holiday	nofio	(to) swim
moyn	(to) want	y	the
dysgu	(to) learn	môr	sea
Cymraeg	Welsh	bob dydd	every day
Croeso	Welcome	gweld	(to) see
i	to	theatr	theater
Abertawe	Swansea	ffilmiau	films
byw	(to) live	wrth gwrs	of course
ers	for, since	chwilio	(to) look for,
pum mlynedd	five years		(to)search
gweithio	(to) work	achau'r teulu	family tree
ydw	yes (I am)	popeth	everything
ydw	I am	dewch!	come!
yn	in	gyda fi	with me

YMARFERION: EXERCISES:

1. Read the Welsh aloud, several times.
2. Cover the English side. Translate the Welsh. Check after each sentence, then attempt it all. Do this several times.
3. Cover the Welsh side. Translate the English. Check after each sentence, then attempt it all. Do this several times.
4. Make up as many sensible sentences as you can, selecting words from each column,

   e.g. Rydw i'n hoffi mynd i'r llyfrgell (*I like going to the library*)
   Mae hi'n hoffi gweithio yn Abertawe (*She likes working in Swansea*)

68

Rydw i'n (*I*)	hoffi	nofio gweld ffilmiau mynd	yn y môr yn y sinema i'r theatr ar wyliau i'r llyfrgell
Mae hi'n (*She*)		gweithio dysgu Cymraeg byw	yn y llyfrgell yn America yn Abertawe
Rydyn ni'n (*We*)			
Maen nhw'n (*They*)			

5. Say what you are: e.g. Nyrs ydw i.
    Here is a short list of occupations:

rheolwr *manager*   ysgrifenyddes *secretary*   athro *teacher* (*male*)
darlithydd *lecturer*   ffermwr *farmer*   athrawes *teacher* (*fem*)
gyrrwr *driver*   technegydd *technician*   siopwr *shopkeeper*
myfyriwr *student*   trydanwr *electrician*   gwraig tŷ *housewife*
clerc *clerk*   pensiynwr *pensioner*   di-waith *unemployed*
gweithiwr cymdeithasol *social worker*

EXTRA GRAMMAR
1. **Familiar and polite forms:**
    'ti' is used for *'you'* (singular) with friends, family and children.
    'chi' is used for *'you'* (singular) with all other people.
    'chi' is also used for *'you'* (plural).
2. **Use of 'yn':**
    'yn' or ''n' is used to introduce nouns and adjectives; it is not used before prepositions:
    Rydw i'n gweld ffilm   *I see a film, I am seeing a film*
    Rydw i ar wyliau   *I am on holidays*
3. **'ydw' and 'ydy' or 'yw'**
    'ydw' is used to link the complement (rather like an = sign) to the subject '*I*' (note that the English word order is reversed):
    Nyrs ydw i   *I am a nurse*
    'ydy' or 'yw' is used to to link the complement to the subject *'he'* or *'she'*:
    Llyfrgellydd yw hi   *she is a librarian*
    Nyrs yw e   *he is a nurse*

69

GWERS PUMP: HOLI'R FFORDD
LESSON FIVE: ASKING THE WAY

Esgusodwch fi	Excuse me	yn syth ymlaen	straight ahead
Ble mae...?	Where is...?	Ydw i?	Am I?
Ble mae'r...?	Where is the...?	Ydych	Yes (you are)
Ewch	Go	ddim	not
i'r chwith	to the left	Diolch yn fawr	Thank you
i'r dde	to the right		very much
chwilio am	look for		

GRAMADEG: GRAMMAR
Asking and answering questions

Form of verb 'to be'	Subject	yn (or 'n)	verb	object	Answer
Ydw	i	'n	dal	tacsi?	Ydych
Do I take a taxi?					*Yes(you do)*
Wyt	ti	'n	dal	bws?	Ydw
Are you taking a bus?					*Yes (I am)*
Ydy	e	'n	dal	trên?	Ydy
Is he catching a train?					*Yes (he is)*
Ydy	hi	'n	mynd â	beic?	Ydy
Is she taking a bike?					*Yes (she is)*
Ydy	Sian	yn	cerdded i'r dre?		Ydy
Is Sian walking to town?					*Yes (she is)*
Ydy'r	plant	yn	dal	y bws?	Ydyn
Are the children catching the bus?					*Yes (they are)*
Ydyn	ni	'n	gwybod y ffordd?		Ydyn
Do we know the way?					*Yes (we do)*
Ydych	chi	'n	gwybod y ffordd?		Ydw
Do you know the way?					*Yes (I do)*
Ydyn	nhw	'n	gwerthu map?		Ydyn
Do they sell a map?					*Yes (they do)*

Alternative form, often heard:

Ydych chi?:   Y'ch chi
uhdich chee   *eech chee*
Ydyn ni?   Y'n ni?
uhdin nee   *een nee*

Answer no:
Na *or*   nag ydw   (*I'm not*)
           nag wyt   (*you're not*)
           nag yw   (*he, she isn't*)
           nag ydyn   (*we're not* or *no they're not*)
           nag ydych (*you're not*)

Mae Janet yn Abertawe. Mae hi'n chwilio am y llyfrgell, ac mae hi ar goll.

Janet:	Esgudosdwch fi. Rydw i ar goll. Ydych chi'n gwybod ble mae'r llyfrgell?
Dafydd:	Ydw, ry'ch chi'n bell iawn. Y'ch chi'n gwybod ble mae'r stryd fawr?
Janet:	Ydw, wrth gwrs.
Dafydd:	Wel, ewch i'r stryd fawr, wedyn ewch i'r chwith, ac wedyn yn syth ymlaen. Wrth y gwesty, trowch i'r chwith eto, ac wedyn i'r dde...
Janet:	Arhoswch! Rydw i ar goll nawr. Ydw i'n troi i'r chwith wrth y gwesty?
Dafydd:	Ydych. Ydych chi'n gwybod ble mae Gwesty Forte?
Janet:	Ydw, wrth y gylchfan.
Dafydd:	Ie, wel, i'r chwith wrth y gwesty, wedyn i'r dde, ar hyd Heol Alexandra, ac mae'r llyfrgell ar y dde.
Janet:	Diolch yn fawr i chi.

Mae Janet yn cerdded i'r stryd fawr, ac wedyn mae hi'n troi i'r chwith. Wedyn maen hi'n troi i'r chwith, ond wedyn mae hi ar goll. Mae Janet yn gweld tacsi. Mae hi'n codi llaw:

Janet:	Tacsi!
Gyrrwr tacsi:	Ie? Ble rydych chi'n mynd?
Janet:	Rwy'n mynd i'r llyfrgell. Ydych chi'n gallu mynd â fi?
Gyrrwr tacsi:	Ydw, wrth gwrs, dim problem. Ydych chi'n dod o Abertawe?
Janet:	Na, rwy'n dod o Vermont.
Gyrrwr tacsi:	Vermont? Jiw, jiw! Mae Dad yn dod o Efrog Newydd! A, dyma ni, wrth y llyfrgell. Tair punt, os gwelwch yn dda.
Janet:	Dyma bum punt. Cadwch y newid.

Yn y llyfrgell:

Janet:	Esgusodwch fi, ydych chi'n gwybod ble mae llyfrau ar achau'r teulu?
Llyfrgellydd:	Ydw. Maen nhw ar y silff ar y dde.

Janet is in Swansea. She is looking for the library, and she is lost.

Janet:	Excuse me. I am lost. Do you know where the library is?
Dafydd:	Yes, you're very far. Do you know where the high street is?
Janet:	Yes, of course.
Dafydd:	Well, go to the high street, then go to the left, and then straight on. By the hotel, turn to the left again, and then to the right...
Janet:	Wait! I'm lost now. Do I turn to the left by the hotel?
Dafydd:	Yes. Do you know where Forte Hotel is?
Janet:	Yes, by the roundabout.
Dafydd:	Yes, well, to the left by the hotel, then to the right, along Alexandra Road, and the library is on the right.
Janet:	Thank you very much.

Janet walks to the high street and then she turns to the left. Then she turns to the left, but then she is lost. Janet sees a taxi. She raises a hand:

Janet:	Taxi!
Taxi driver:	Yes? Where are you going?
Janet:	I'm going to the library. Can you take me?
Taxi driver:	Yes, of course, no problem. Do you come from Swansea?
Janet:	No, I come from Vermont.
Taxi driver:	Vermont? Dear me! Dad comes from New York! Ah! here we are, by the library. Three pounds, please.
Janet:	Here are five pounds. Keep the change.

In the library:

Janet:	Excuse me. Do you know where the books on family trees are?
Librarian:	They are on the shelf on the right.

GEIRFA: VOCABULARY

chwilio am	(to) look for	codi	(to) raise
ar goll	lost	llaw	hand
esgusodwch fi	excuse me	gallu	(to) be able (to)
gwybod	(to) know	problem	problem
yn bell	far	jiw jiw!	dear me!
stryd	street	dyma ni	here we are
fawr	big, high	tair	three
wrth gwrs	of course	punt	pound
ewch	go	cadwch	keep
gwesty	hotel	newid	(to) change
y gylchfan	the roundabout	os gwelwch	please
wrth	by	yn dda	
ar hyd	along	dyma bum	here's £5
diolch yn fawr	thank you	punt	
i chi	very much	silff	shelf
tacsi	taxi		

YMARFERION: EXCERCISES

1. Read the Welsh aloud, several times.
2. Cover the English side. Translate the Welsh. Check after each sentence, then attempt it all. Do this several times.
3. Cover the Welsh side. Translate the English. Check after each sentence, then attempt it all. Do this several times.
   DO THE ABOVE THREE EXCERCISES WITH ALL THE LESSONS TO COME. THESE INSTRUCTIONS WILL NOT BE REPEATED.
4. Make up as many sensible questions as you can, selecting words from each column,
   e.g. Ydych chi'n gwybod ble mae'r llyfrgell? (*Do you know where the library is?*)

Ydych chi'n (*Do you know...*)	gwybod	ble mae'r	llyfrgell sinema
Ydy'r tacsi'n (*Is the taxi going to...*)	mynd	i'r	theatr gwesty

5. Answer yes to the above questions.

6. Translate:
Go to the left
Go to the right
Go straight ahead
Go to the high street
Go to the cinema
Go to the library
Go to the hotel

7. Janet is in the cirle marked X. Tell her how she can get to the places mentioned.

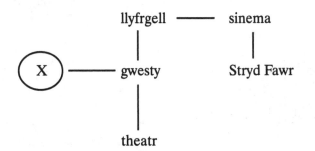

e.g. Ewch yn syth ymlaen i'r gwesty.
Wrth y gwesty ewch i'r chwith i'r llyfrgell.

EXTRA GRAMMAR
1. **The article in Welsh**
There is no word for 'a' or 'an'. It is simply left out, so 'theatr' means *'theater'* or *'a theater'*.
'The' is usually 'y': y theatr; y sinema; y stryd.
Before vowels 'y' becomes 'yr': yr ysgol (*the school*); yr afon (*the river*); yr afal (*the apple*).
After vowels 'y' and 'yr' become ' 'r ': Mae'r theatr yn y stryd fawr (*the theater is in the high street*); i'r gwesty (*to the hotel*).

2. **Translating present tense verbs:**
'Ydych chi' can mean *'do you'* or *'are you'*:
Ydych chi'n dod?   *Are you coming?*
Ydych chi'n hoffi coffi   *Do you like coffee?*
Forms of the present tense can also be translated with or without using the verb 'to be' in English:
Rwy'n cerdded   *I walk* or *I am walking*

75

GWERS CHWECH: BETH SY'N DIGWYDD?
LESSON SIX: WHAT'S ON?

Beth sy yn y theatr?	What's in the theater?	coleg	college
y dafarn	the pub	prifysgol	university
y ganolfan hamdden	the leisure center	wn i ddim	I don't know
		ffilm	film
yr eglwys	the church	drama	drama
y neuadd	the hall	cyngerdd	concert
neuadd y dref	the town hall	arddangosfa	exhibition
ysgol	school	nofio	swimming
		hoffi	(to) like

GRAMADEG: GRAMMAR
The negative sentence:

Negative of verb'to be'	Subject	negative + 'yn'	verb	object
Dw	i	ddim yn	hoffi	drama

I don't like drama

Dwyt	ti	ddim yn	hoffi	ffilmiau

You don't like films

Dyw	e	ddim yn	hoffi	cyngerdd

He doesn't like a concert

Dyw	hi	ddim yn	hoffi	nofio

She doesn't like swimming

Dyw	Sian	ddim yn	hoffi	yfed

Sian doesn't like drinking

Dyw'r	plant	ddim yn	hoffi	chwarae

The children don't like playing

Dy'n	ni	ddim yn	hoffi	drama

We don't like drama

Dy'ch	chi	ddim yn	hoffi	cerdded

You don't like walking

Dy'n	nhw	ddim yn	hoffi	dal bws

They don't like to catch a bus

Alternative forms and pronunciations:

Dw i ddim:	Dydw i ddim
doo ee thim	*duhdoo ee thim*
Dyw e ddim:	Dydy e ddim
dioo eh thim	*duhdee eh thim*
Dyw hi ddim:	Dydy hi ddim
dioo hee thim	*duhdee hee thim*
Dy'n ni ddim:	Dydyn ni ddim:
deen nee thim	*duhdin nee thim*
Dy'ch chi ddim:	Dydych chi ddim
deech chee thim	*duhdich chee thim*
Dy'n nhw ddim:	Dydyn nhw ddim
deen nhoo thim	*duhdin nhoo thim*

Mae Janet yn y llyfrgell. Mae hi'n gofyn beth sy yn Abertawe heno. Mae hi'n moyn mynd i'r theatr neu i'r sinema.

Janet:	Diolch yn fawr am eich help.
Llyfrgellydd:	Croeso.
Janet:	Wel, rwy'n chwilio am wybodaeth am heno. Rwy'n moyn mynd i'r sinema, neu i'r theatr. Oes theatr yn Abertawe?
Llyfrgellydd:	Oes, mae tair theatr yma. Theatr y Grand yw'r theatr fwyaf. Mae Theatr Dylan Thomas wrth y Marina, ac mae Theatr Taliesin yn y coleg.
Janet:	Ydych chi'n gwybod beth sy yn y theatrau heno?
Llyfrgellydd:	Na, dw i ddim yn gwybod, ond mae'r papur lleol gyda fi. Un funud. A, dyma fe. Mae drama gan Alan Ayckbourn yn y Grand ac mae ffilm yn Theatr Taliesin. Ydych chi'n hoffi Alan Ayckbourn?
Janet:	Na, dw i ddim yn hoffi Ayckbourn. Pa ffilm sy yn y theatr?
Llyfrgellydd:	Dw i ddim yn siŵr. Ffilm o Rwsia, rwy'n credu, *Rhyfel a Heddwch*. Ydych chi'n hoffi'r nofel?
Janet:	Na, dw i ddim yn hoffi'r nofel - mae'n hir iawn. Oes sinema yn Abertawe?
Llyfrgellydd:	Oes, wrth gwrs. Mae dwy sinema yma, ac mae sawl sgrîn yn y ddwy sinema.
Janet:	Oes ffilmiau da yn y sinemâu?
Llyfrgellydd:	Na, does dim llawer o ffilmiau da yma. O, un funud, mae ffilm dda yn yr Odeon: ffilm James Bond.
Janet:	Dw i ddim yn hoffi James Bond! Oes cyngerdd yn Abertawe heno?
Llyfrgellydd:	Oes, mae cyngerdd yn Neuadd y Brangwyn. Nawfed symffoni Beethoven.
Janet:	Hyfryd! O'r diwedd. Ydw i'n gallu cael tocynnau dros y ffôn?
Llyfrgellydd:	Dw i ddim yn siŵr. Dyma'r ffôn.

Mae Janet yn ffonio.

Janet:	Prynhawn da.... rydw i'n moyn un tocyn i'r cyngerdd heno... Deg punt? Na, dw i ddim yn moyn talu deg punt... Wyth punt? Iawn.... Un tocyn wyth punt, os gwelwch chi'n dda.

Janet is in the library. She is asking what is (on) in Swansea tonight.
She wants to go the the theater or to the cinema.

Janet:	Thank you for your help.
Librarian:	Not at all. .
Janet:	Well, I'm looking for information for tonight. I want to go to the cinema, or to the theater. Is there a theater in Swansea?
Librarian:	Yes, there are three theaters here. The Grand Theater is the biggest theater. Dylan Thomas Theater is by the Marina, and Taliesin Theater is in the college.
Janet:	Do you know what is in the theaters tonight?
Librarian:	No, I don't know, but I have the local paper. One moment. Ah, here it is. There is a play by Alan Ayckbourn in the Grand and there's a film in Taliesin Theater. Do you like Alan Ayckbourn?
Janet:	No, I don't like Ayckbourn. Which film is in the theater?
Librarian:	I'm not sure. A film from Russia, I believe, *War and Peace*. Do you like the novel?
Janet:	No, I don't like the novel - it's very long. Is there a cinema in Swansea?
Librarian:	Yes, of course. There are two cinemas here, and there are several screens in the two cinemas.
Janet:	Are there good films in the cinemas?
Librarian:	No, there aren't many good films here. Oh, one moment, there is a good film in the Odeon: a James Bond film.
Janet:	I don't like James Bond! Is there a concert in Swansea tonight?
Librarian:	Yes, there is a concert in the Brangwyn Hall. Beethoven'sninth symphony.
Janet:	Lovely! At last. Can I get tickets over the phone?
Librarian:	I'm not sure. Here's the phone.

Janet phones.

Janet:	Good afternoon... I want one ticket for the concert to night... £10? No, I don't want to pay £10... £8? Fine... One ticket for £8, please.

GEIRFA: VOCABULARY

beth sy	what is	iawn	very
heno	tonight	pa	which
neu	or	o Rwsia	from Russia
am	for	rhyfel	war
croeso	welcome, not at all	heddwch	peace
gofynnwch	ask	nofel	novel
am wybodaeth	for information	hir	long
am heno	about tonight	dwy	two
oes? oes	is there? yes	sawl	several
tair	three	[followed by singular noun]	
[with feminine nouns]		sgrîn	screen
fwyaf	biggest	ffilmiau	films
coleg	college	dda	good
theatrau	theaters	siŵr	sure
papur	paper	cyngerdd	concert
lleol	local	nawfed	ninth
un funud	one minute, one moment	symffoni	symphony
		un	one
dyma fe	here it is	o'r diwedd	at last
gan	by	tocyn	ticket
does dim	there isn't	tocynnau	tickets
dim byd	nothing	dros y ffôn	over the phone
wyth punt	£8		
hoff	fond	deg punt	£10
hyfryd	pleasant, lovely	talu	(to) pay

YMARFERION: EXCERCISES

1. Make as many sentences as possible, selecting words from each column:

Dydw i	ddim yn	hoffi	ffilmiau
Dyw hi			dramâu
Dy'n ni			nofelau
Dy'ch chi			cyngherddau

2. Translate the following:

Rwy'n hoffi'r nofel, ond dw i ddim yn hoffi'r ffilm.
Rwy'n hoffi cerdded, ond dw i ddim yn hoffi nofio.
Rwy'n hoffi coffi, ond dw i ddim yn hoffi te.
Rwy'n hoffi Beethoven, ond dw i ddim yn hoffi Mozart.

3. Make up similar sentences to those in 2 above, using the following words:

Schubert	Brahms
nofelau	dramâu
Vermont	Abertawe
ffilmiau James Bond	ffilmiau Spielberg
dal bws	cerdded

EXTRA GRAMMAR

1. THERE IS / THERE ARE

'Mae' on its own means *'there is'* or *'there are'*:

Mae drama yn y theatr.   *There's a drama in the theater.*

'Oes?' asks the question 'is there?' or 'are there?':

Oes ffilm yn y sinema?   *Is there a film in the cinema?*

The answer *'yes'* is 'oes':

Oes, mae ffilm yn y sinema. *Yes, there is a film in the cinema.*

The answer *'no'* is 'na' or 'nag oes':

Na, does dim ffilm yno.   *No, there's no film there.*

2. EMPHASIS

To emphasize a noun, put it at the start of the sentence, and use 'sy' for 'is':

Ayckbourn sy yn y theatr. *It's Ayckbourn who's in the theater.*

3. NUMBERS

Numbers are followed by singular nouns:

un caffe;   pum punt;   wyth potel

4. PLURALS

Many Welsh words form their plural by adding '-au' or '-iau' (pronounced 'eh' and 'yeh'):

nofel	nofelau	theatr	theatrau
cyngerdd	cyngherddau	ffilm	ffilmiau

Note these two:

drama	dramâu	sinema	sinemâu

GWERS SAITH: AROS NOSON
LESSON SEVEN: STAYING THE NIGHT

gwesty	hotel	tŷ bach	toilet
gwely	bed	papur tŷ bach	toilet paper
llety	lodgings	sebon	soap
chwilio am	(to) look for	tywel	towel
un noson	one night	cawod	shower
wythnos	week	dillad gwely	bed clothes
gwely a	bed and	bwyta	(to) eat
brecwast	breakfast	cadw lle	(to) book a
cinio	dinner, lunch		room
aros am	(to) stay for	yfed	(to) drink
swper	supper	cês	case
diod	drink	lle parcio	parking space
ystafell	room		
ystafell ymolchi	bathroom		

GRAMADEG - GRAMMAR

'*I have*' (possess) or '*I have got*' is translated using the preposition 'gyda' :

I have a car	Mae car gyda fi	literally '*There is a car with me*'

'Gyda' is often shortened to ' 'da'.

Mae	car	'da	fi	*car*
	cawod		ti	*shower*
	ystafell wely		fe	*bedroom*
	cês		hi	*case*
	lle parcio		ni	*parking space*
Oes	bwyd da		chi	*good food*
	bar		nhw	*bar*

To ask if someone has something, change the 'Mae' to 'Oes':

Oes bar 'da chi?	*Have you got a bar?*
Oes	*Yes*
Na	*No*

Mae Janet yn cyrraedd gwesty.

Janet: Noswaith dda.

Mr Jones; Noswaith dda. Ga i helpu?

Janet: Rydw i'n chwilio am lety.

Mr Jones: Am sawl noson?

Janet: Am saith noson.

Mr Jones: Ystafell sengl neu ddwbl?

Janet: Wi'n chwilio am ystafell sengl. Oes ystafell sengl 'da chi?

Mr Jones: Oes, ac mae tŷ bach a chawod yn yr ystafell wely.

Janet: Da iawn. Beth yw cost yr ystafell?

Mr Jones: Pymtheg punt y nos.

Janet: Ydy'r pris yn cynnwys brecwast?

Mr Jones: Ydy. Mae brecwast Cymreig llawn yma.

Janet: Diolch. Ga i'r ystafell am wythnos?

Mr Jones: Croeso. Oes cesys 'da chi?

Janet: Oes, mae un ces 'da fi.

Mr Jones: Ga i helpu?

Janet: Croeso, diolch. Oes bar 'da chi?

Mr Jones: Oes, mae bar 'da ni, ac mae ystafell fwyta 'da ni - ryn ni'n gwneud cinio yn y dydd a swper yn y nos.

Janet: Ble ydw i'n gallu gadael y car?

Mr Jones: Ar y stryd yn y dydd, ond mae lle parcio 'da ni, yn y cefn. Unrhyw beth arall?

Janet: Ga i'r allwedd i'r ystafell, os gwelwch yn dda?

Mr Jones: Wrth gwrs. Dyma fe.

Janet: Ydy'r bar ar agor?

Janet arrives at an hotel.

Janet: Good evening.

Mr Jones: Good evening. May I help?

Janet: I'm looking for lodgings.

Mr Jones: For how many nights?

Janet: For seven nights.

Mr Jones: Single room or a double?

Janet: I'm looking for a single room. Have you got a single room?

Mr Jones: Yes, and there is a toilet and a shower in the bedroom.

Janet: Very good. What is the cost of the room?

Mr Jones: Fifteen pounds a night.

Janet: Does the price include breakfast?

Mr Jones: Yes. There is a full Welsh breakfast here.

Janet: Thanks. May I have the room for a week?

Mr Jones: Welcome. Have you got suitcases?

Janet: Yes, I have one suitcase.

Mr Jones: May I help?

Janet: Welcome, thanks. Have you got a bar?

Mr Jones: Yes, we have a bar, and we have a dining room - we make lunch in the day and supper in the evening.

Janet: Where can I leave the car?

Mr Jones: On the street in the day, but we have a parking space, in the back. Anything else?

Janet: May I have the key to the room, please?

Mr Jones: Of course. Here it is.

Janet: Is the bar open?

GEIRFA: VOCABULARY

sawl	how many	ystafell wely	bedroom
noson	night	bar	bar
sengl	single	yn y dydd	during the day
dwbl, ddwbl	double	yn y cefn	in the back
cost	cost	unrhyw	any
pris	price	unrhyw beth	anything
cynnwys	(to) include	arall	else, other
Cymreig	Welsh	allwedd	key
llawn	full	croeso	welcome
cesys	cases	dyma	here is
ystafell fwyta	dining room	dyma fe	here it is

YMARFERION: EXCERCISES

1. Say that you have the following things:
    e.g bag   Mae bag 'da fi.   *I have a bag.*
    car;   llety;   ystafell sengl;   gwely dwbl;   lle parcio

2. Answer the following questions:
    a)   Oes car 'da chi?
    b)   Oes cawod 'da chi yn yr ystafell wely?
    c)   Oes gwely dwbl 'da chi?
    d)   Oes gwely sengl 'da chi?

3. Translate the following:
    I am looking for a single room.
    For how many nights?
    For one night.
    May I have a double room?
    Has it got a toilet?
    Yes, and a shower.
    May I have the room, please?

EXTRA GRAMMAR

Other phrases using 'da:

I have a headache	Mae pen tost 'da fi
I have a cold	Mae annwyd 'da fi
I'd rather go	Mae'n well 'da fi fynd
I'd rather an orange	Mae'n well 'da fi oren

GWERS WYTH: YN Y BAR
LESSON EIGHT: IN THE BAR

peint	pint	cadair	chair
cwrw	beer	jin	gin
gwin	wine	tonic	tonic
gwydraid o	a glass of	sieri	sherry
gwin gwyn	white wine	iâ	ice
gwin coch	red wine	dŵr	water
hanner peint	half a pint	potel	bottle

GRAMADEG: GRAMMAR : Feminine and masculine nouns

All nouns in Welsh are either masculine and feminine, e.g.

MASCULINE		FEMININE	
dyn	man	menyw	woman
bachgen	boy	merch	girl
tad	father	mam	mother
tad-cu	grandfather	mam-gu	grandmother
brawd	brother	chwaer	sister
cefnder	cousin (m)	cyfnither	cousin (f)

Here are some others:

tŷ	house	gardd	garden
car	car	ffenestr	window
teledu	television	stryd	street
pentref	village	tref	town
bwrdd	table	desg	desk
parc	park	dinas	city
llyfr	book	ffilm	film
trên	train	llong	ship
tocyn	ticket	gorsaf	station
gwesty	hotel	ystafell	room

88

The first letter of feminine nouns can change ('mutate') after the definite article ('the') - y, yr or 'r. These are the letters that can change. This change is called '**soft mutation**':

c	>	g	cath	(*cat*)	y gath	
p	>	p	pont	(*bridge*)	y bont	
t	>	d	tref	(*town*)	y dref	
g	>	/	gardd	(*garden*)	yr ardd	(the 'g' disappears)
b	>	f	basged	(*basket*)	y fasged	
d	>	dd	dinas	(*city*)	y ddinas	
m	>	f	mam	(*mother*)	y fam	

Two other letters can also change in other circumstances (to be discussed at the end of this lesson):

ll   >   l   rh   >   r

Mae Janet yn y bar yn y gwesty. Mae hi'n edrych ar y prisiau.

Janet: Peint o gwrw, un bunt saith deg ceiniog; gwydraid o win gwyn, un bunt chwe deg ceiniog; sieri, un bunt pedwar deg ceiniog; jin a tonic, un bunt chwe deg ceiniog; peint o Guinness, dwy bunt; ...

Barman: Ga i helpu? Beth ydych chi'n moyn?

Janet: Sudd lemwn, efallai, sudd oren, sudd afal. Mae gormod o ddewis yma. Dŵr efallai. Oes dŵr o Gymru 'da chi?

Barman: Oes, mae dŵr Tŷ Nant 'da ni. Ydych chi'n moyn potel o ddŵr?

Janet: Dw i ddim yn siŵr. Faint yw'r gwin coch?

Barman: Un bunt, chwe deg ceiniog.

Janet: Faint yw hanner peint o gwrw?

Barman: Naw deg ceiniog.

Janet: A faint yw seidir?

Barman: Dwy bunt y peint, neu hanner peint am bunt.

Janet: Pa fath o gwrw sy 'da chi?

Barman: Cwrw melyn, cwrw mwyn, cwrw tywyll...

Janet: Hanner peint o gwrw mwyn, os gwelwch yn dda, gyda thipyn bach o lemwnêd.

Barman: Naw deg ceiniog, os gwelwch yn dda.

Janet: Dyma bunt.

Barman: A dyma ddeg ceiniog o newid. Iechyd da i chi!

Janet: Iechyd da! Ydych chi'n gwerthu bwyd?

Barman: Ydyn. Ryn ni'n gwerthu creision, cnau, a rholiau. Rholiau ham a salad, ffowlyn, caws a salad.

Janet: Ydych chi'n gwneud bwyd twym?

Barman: Ydyn. Cyw yn y fasged, pysgod a sglodion, lasagne a salad.

Janet: Faint yw'r bwyd?

Barman: Tair punt pum deg am fwyd twym. Punt pum deg yw'r rholiau.

Janet: Cyw yn y fasged os gwelwch yn dda. Dyma bum punt.

Barman: Un bunt pum deg o newid.

Janet is in the bar in the hotel. She's looking at the prices.

Janet: A pint of beer, £1.70p; a glass of white wine, £1.60p; sherry, £1.40p; gin and tonic, £1.60p; a pint of Guinness, £2;...

Barman: May I help? What do you want?

Janet: Lemon juice, perhaps, orange juice, apple juice. There is too much choice here. Water, perhaps. Have you got water from Wales?

Barman: Yes, we have Tŷ Nant water. Do you want a bottle of water?

Janet: I'm not sure. How much is the red wine?

Barman: £1.60p.

Janet: How much is half a pint of beer?

Barman: 90p.

Janet: And how much is cider?

Barman: £2 a pint, or half a pint for a £1.

Janet: What kind of beer do you have?

Barman: Bitter beer, mild beer, dark beer...

Janet: Half a pint of mild beer, please, with a little lemonade.

Barman: 90p, please.

Janet: Here is a pound.

Barman: And here is 10p change. Good health to you!

Janet: Good health! Do you sell food?

Barman: Yes, We sell crisps, nuts and rolls. Ham and salad rolls, chicken, cheese and salad.

Janet: Do you do hot food?

Barman: Yes. Chicken in the basket, fish and chips, lasagne and salad.

Janet: How much is the food?

Barman: £3.50 for hot food. The rolls are £1.50.

Janet: Chicken in the basket, please. Here are five pounds.

Barman: £1.50 change.

GEIRFA: VOCABULARY

sudd (m)	juice	tipyn bach o	a little (of)
lemwn (m)	lemon	iechyd da!	Good health!
oren (m)	orange		Cheers!
afal (m/f)	apple	gwerthu	(to) sell
dŵr (m)	water	bwyd (m)	food
Cymru (f)	Wales	creision	crisps
potel (f)	bottle	rholiau	rolls
hanner (m)	half	ham (m)	ham
hanner peint	half a pint	salad (m)	salad
cwrw (m)	beer	ffowlyn (m)	chicken
melyn	yellow	caws (m)	cheese
mwyn	mild	twym	warm
tywyll	dark	basged (f)	basket
newid	change		

YMARFERION: EXCERCISES

1. Say you would like:
a glass of wine;	half a pint of beer;
a bottle of water;	a pint of cider;
a glass of white wine;	apple juice;
orange juice;	a glass or red wine;
half a pint of Guinness	

    e.g. Rwy'n moyn peint o gwrw, os gwelwch yn dda
    or Ga i beint o gwrw, os gwelwch yn dda?

2. Give the following prices:
£5	£2.50	£3.50	£7.00
£10	£1.50	£8.00	£9.00

EXTRA GRAMMAR
Soft Mutations:
The letter changes mentioned above occur often. They change in
the following circumstances and in many others. If you do not mutate, or if you mutate incorrectly, you will still be understood.

1. Feminine nouns after 'y', 'yr' and ' 'r' (*the*).
2. After 'dau' (m) , 'dwy' (f) (*two*).
3. After 'o' (*of*).
4. After 'am' (*for, at*).
5. After 'dyma' (*here is, here are*).
6. Feminine nouns after 'un' (*one*).
7. After 'ga i' (*may I have*).

GWERS NAW: AMSER BRECWAST
LESSON NINE: BREAKFAST TIME

bara (m)	bread	marmalêd (m)	marmalade
tost (m)	toast	cig moch (m)	bacon
coffi (m)	coffee	soser (f)	saucer
te (m)	tea	cwpan (m/f)	cup
mêl (m)	honey	cwpaned o de	a cup of tea
jam (m)	jam	cwpaned o goffi	a cup of coffee
tebot (m)	teapot	plât (m)	plate
llaeth (m)	milk	fforc (f)	ffork
siwgr (m)	sugar	cyllell (f)	knife
wy (m)	egg	llwy (f)	spoon
halen (m)	salt	wy wedi'i ferwi	boiled egg
pupur (m)	pepper	wy wedi'i ffrio	fried egg
jwg (m)	jug	selsig	saugages
llwy de	teaspoon	tomato	tomato

GRAMADEG: GRAMMAR
Adjectives
Adjectives in Welsh usually follow the noun

e.g.   brecwast mawr   *big breakfast*

Adjectives mutate after feminine nouns

e.g.   llwy fawr   *a big spoon*

Adjectives mutate after 'yn' as part of the verb 'be'

e.g.   Mae'r brecwast yn fawr   *The breakfast is big*

'Hen' (*old*) is used before the noun, and the noun is mutated:

e.g.   Hen dŷ   *old house*

Adverbs
To form adverbs, simply put 'yn' before the adjective and mutate:

e.g.   da   *good*;   yn dda   *well*

Colours:

gwyn	white	du	black
coch	red	brown	brown
melyn	yellow	llwyd	grey
glas	blue	oren	orange
gwyrdd	green	pinc	pink
porffor	purple	golau	light
aur	gold	tywyll	dark
arian	silver		

Mae Janet yn codi am saith o'r gloch, ac mae hi'n cael brecwast yn y gwesty.

Gweinydd: Bore da! Ydych chi'n barod i gael brecwast?

Janet: Bore da! Beth sy i frecwast?

Gweinydd: Mae digon o ddewis. Ydych chi'n moyn brecwast oer neu dwym?

Janet: Brecwast twym, os gwelwch yn dda.

Gweinydd: Wel, mae 'da ni wy, cig moch, selsig, tomatos, tost.

Janet: Wy wedi'i ffrio, os gwelwch yn dda, cig moch, tost bara brown a mêl, ond dim selsig, a dim tomatos - a digon o halen.

Gweinydd: Ydych chi'n moyn te neu goffi?

Janet: Coffi du, os gwelwch yn dda... Mae'r plât yma'n frwnt.

Gweinydd: O, mae'n flin 'da fi. Wi'n mynd i nôl plât arall.

Janet: Ac mae'r fforc yma'n frwnt hefyd.

Gweinydd: Wi'n mynd i nôl fforc lân nawr.

Janet: Diolch! Oes papur newyddion 'da chi?

Gweinydd: Oes, dyma fe.

Janet: Does dim llwy de 'da fi.

Gweinydd: Mae'n flin 'da fi. Dyma lwy de i chi.

Janet: Oes llaeth 'da chi?

Gweinydd: Oes, mae llaeth yn y jwg glas, ac mae *Corn Flakes* yn y fowlen binc ar y bwrdd.

Janet: Hyfryd, diolch yn fawr.

Gweinydd: Unrhyw beth arall?

Janet: Y bil, os gwelwch yn dda.

Gweinydd: Does dim bil - rydych chi'n talu am wely a brecwast.

Janet gets up at seven o'clock, and she's having breakfast in the hotel.

Waiter: Good morning! Are you ready to have breakfast?

Janet: Good morning! What's for breakfast?

Waiter: There's plenty of choice. Do you want a cold or warm breakfast?

Janet: A warm breakfast, please.

Waiter: Well, we have egg, bacon, sausages, tomatoes, toast.

Janet: A fried egg, please, bacon, brown bread toast and honey, but no sausages and no tomatoes - and plenty of salt.

Waiter: Do you want tea or coffee?

Janet: Black coffee, please... This plate is dirty.

Waiter: Oh, I'm sorry. I'm going to get another plate.

Janet: And this fork is dirty too.

Waiter: I'm going to get a clean fork now.

Janet: Thanks! Do you have a newspaper?

Waiter: Yes, here it is.

Janet: I haven't got a teaspoon.

Waiter: I'm sorry. Here's a teaspoon for you.

Janet: Have you got milk?

Waiter: Yes, there's milk in the blue jug, and there are *Corn Flakes* in the pink bowl on the table.

Janet: Lovely, thanks.

Waiter: Anything else?

Janet: The bill, please.

Waiter: There's no bill - you're paying for bed and breakfast.

GEIRFA: VOCABULARY

cael	have, get	bowlen(f)	bowl
brecwast (m)	breakfast	hyfryd	lovely, pleasant
i frecwast	for breakfast	bil (m)	bill
oer	cold	talu	(to) pay
twym	warm, hot	gwely (m)	bed
brwnt	dirty	glân	clean
mae'n flin	I'm sorry	papur	newspaper
'da fi		newyddion	

YMARFERION: EXCERCISES

1. Translate:
   What's for breakfast?
   May I have a cup of black coffee?
   I want brown bread, please.
   Have you got any milk?
   May I have bacon, toast and egg?

2. Link words in the left column to adjectives in the right:

gwin	glân
brecwast	gwyn
bara	twym
plât	brown

3. Mutate the following adjectives after the feminine nouns:
   llwy + glân
   ffilm + da
   fforc + brwnt

EXTRA GRAMMAR
Comparison of adjectives:
1. Long form
as ... as mor .... â
   mor lân â   *as clean as* (note soft mutation after 'mor')
more mwy; *than* na
   mwy glân na   *cleaner than*
most mwya
   mwya glân   *most clean*
2. Short form
...er ...ach
   glanach na   *cleaner than*
...est ...af
   glanaf   *cleanest*

| GWERS DEG: | CAEL CINIO |
| LESSON TEN: | HAVING LUNCH (DINNER) |

caffe (m)	café	brithyll (m)	trout
tŷ bwyta (m)	restaurant	lleden (f)	plaice (a flat
bwydlen (f)	menu		fish)
cig (m)	meat	sewin (m)	sewin (river
eidion (m)	beef		salmon)
oen (m)	lamb	caws (m)	cheese
cyw (m)	chicken	menyn (m)	butter
ffowlyn (m)	chicken	ffrwythau (pl)	fruit
porc (m)	pork	afalau (pl)	apples
llysiau (pl)	vegetables	orennau (pl)	oranges
tatws (pl)	potatoes	gellyg (pl)	pears
sglodion (pl)	chips	grawnwin (pl)	grapes
bresych (pl)	cabbage	banana (m)	banana
moron (pl)	carrots	eirin (pl)	plums
pys (pl)	peas	eirin gwlanog	peaches
letys (pl)	lettuce	pwdin (m)	sweet, pudding
pysgod (pl)	fish	cwstard (m)	custard
eog (m)	salmon	reis (m)	rice
penfras (m)	cod	hufen iâ (m)	ice cream
		tarten (f)	tart, pie

GRAMADEG: GRAMMAR
Past tense: saying you have done something
This is much easier in Welsh than in English. Simply *replace* the 'yn' or ' 'n' used with the present tense by 'wedi':

-yn-	-wedi-
Mae e'n mynd *He is going*	Mae e wedi mynd *He has gone*
Rwy'n yfed *I am drinking*	Rwy wedi yfed *I have drunk*
Ydy e'n dod *Is he coming?*	Ydy e wedi dod? *Has he come?*
Ydy hi'n bwyta? *Is she eating?*	Ydy hi wedi bwyta? *Has she eaten?*

In English, the verb has to change: eat > eaten; drink > drunk. This does not happen in Welsh.

Dyw e ddim wedi cyrraedd	*He hasn't arrived*
Maen nhw wedi gorffen	*They have finished*
Dy'n ni ddim wedi codi	*We haven't got up*
Ry'ch chi wedi mwynhau	*You have enjoyed*

Mae Janet a Mari ei ffrind wedi mynd i'r tŷ bwyta i gael cinio. Maen nhw wedi eistedd wrth y bwrdd, ac maen nhw'n edrych ar y fwydlen.

Janet: Wel, Mari, beth wyt ti eisiau i ginio?

Mari: Rwy wedi bwyta gormod i frecwast, ac ry'n ni wedi cael coffi. Dw i ddim eisiau bwyta llawer.

Janet: Ond mae rhaid i ti gael rhywbeth.

Mari: O'r gorau. Fe ga i bysgodyn.

Gweinydd: Ydych chi wedi dewis eto?

Janet: Na, dw i ddim wedi dewis eto.

Gweinydd: Ydych chi am gael rhywbeth i yfed?

Janet: Gwin coch os gwelwch yn dda. Wyt ti wedi dewis, Mari?

Mari: Wi eisiau cael sudd oren.

Gweinydd: Beth hoffech chi gael i ddechrau?

Janet: Dim byd i ddechrau. Ry'n ni wedi bwyta gormod i frecwast. Ond hoffwn i gael cyw a llysiau.

Gweinydd: Cyw wedi'i rostio?

Janet: Ie, os gwelwch yn dda.

Gweinydd: Tatws wedi berwi?

Janet: Na, sglodion, os gwelwch yn dda.

Gweinydd: Pwdin?

Janet: Hufen iâ a ffrwythau.

Gweinydd: A chithau?

Mari: Eog mewn saws gwyn, os gwelwch yn dda, a thatws newydd.

Gweinydd: Ac i bwdin?

Mari: Tarten afalau, os gwelwch yn dda.

Janet: O daro, ry'n ni'n mynd i fwyta gormod, unwaith eto.

Janet and her friend have gone into a restaurant to have lunch. They have sat by the table, and they are looking at the menu.

Janet: Wel, Mari, what do you want for lunch?

Mari: I have eaten too much for breakfast, and we have had coffee. I don't want to eat a lot.

Janet: But you must have something.

Mari: All right. I shall have a fish.

Waiter: Have you chosen yet?

Janet: No, I haven't chosen yet.

Waiter: Do you want to have something to drink?

Janet: Red wine please. Have you chosen, Mari?

Mari: I want to have orange juice.

Waiter: What would you like to start?

Janet: Nothing to start. We have eaten too much for breakfast. But I would like to have chicken and vegetables.

Waiter: Roasted chicken?

Janet: Yes, please.

Waiter: Boiled potatoes?

Janet: No, chips, please.

Waiter: Sweet?

Janet: Ice cream and fruit.

Waiter: And you?

Mari: Salmon in white sauce, please, and new potatoes.

Waiter: And for sweet?

Mari: Apple pie, please.

Janet: O dear, we are going to eat too much, once again.

GEIRFA: VOCABULARY

i ginio	for dinner	hoffech	you would like,
i frecwast	for breakfast		would you like?
i de	for tea	dim byd	nothing
eisiau	want	hoffwn	I would like
rhywbeth	something	dechrau	start
fe	no meaning;	rhostio	(to) roast
	it confirms the verb	berwi	(to) boil
fe ga i	I'll have	chithau	you (with
dewis	choose		emphasis)
eto	yet, again	saws (m)	sauce
unwaith eto	once again	newydd	new
		daro	dear

YMARFERION: EXCERCISES

1. Make up sentences taking words from each column:

Rwy Mae hi	wedi	bwyta yfed	tost te cyw sglodion wy wedi'i ffrio selsig	i frecwast i ginio

2. Say what you have had today, for breakfast and for lunch.
   e.g. I frecwast, rwy wedi bwyta tost a jam. Rwy wedi yfed coffi.

EXTRA GRAMMAR

1. **Would like:**
   Note how the verb 'hoffi' can be used to mean 'would like:

hoffwn i	*I would like*	hoffen ni	*we would like*
hoffet ti	*you would like*	hoffech chi	*you would like*
hoffai fe	*he would like*	hoffen nhw	*they would like*
hoffai hi	*she would like*		

   hoffech chi? *would you like?*   hoffwn   *yes (I would like)*

All these are followed by **soft mutation:**
Hoffwn i fynd - *I would like to go*

2. **Another mutation: aspirate mutation after 'a':**

The following changes occur to the first letters of nouns
after 'a' (and) and also after 'â' (with), 'tri' (three) and 'chwe'
(six):

c	>	ch	tatws a chyw	*potatoes and chicken*
p	>	ph	bresych a phys	*cabbage and peas*
t	>	th	coffi a the	*coffee and tea*

tri chi	*three dogs*
chwe phlentyn	*six children*
tri thŷ	*three houses*
chwe phunt	*six pounds*

GWERS UN DEG UN: SIOPA
LESSON ELEVEN: SHOPPING

dillad (pl)	clothes	bag (m)	bag
esgidiau (pl)	shoes	bag llaw hand	bag
sanau (pl)	socks, stockings	cês (m)	case
trowsus (m)	trousers	llestri (pl)	dishes
sgert (f)	skirt	anrheg (f)	present
siwt (f)	suit	llyfr (m)	book
siaced (f)	jacket	bwyd (m)	food
blows (f)	blouse	bisgedi (pl)	biscuits
bronglwm (m)	bra	siocled (m)	chocolate
crys (m)	shirt	llwy garu (f)	lovespoon
tei (m)	tie	darlun (m)	picture
trons (m)	underpants	calendr (m)	calendar
nicyrs (m)	knickers	syniad (m)	idea
sgarff (f)	scarf		

GRAMADEG: GRAMMAR

Plurals: There are many ways of forming plurals of Welsh words.
Here are some common endings added to words:

-au	**-iau**	**-ion**
gwely/au *beds*	darlun/iau *pictures*	dyn/ion *men*
calendr/au *calendars*	llun/iau *pictures*	anrheg/ion *presents*
llyfr/au *books*	bag/iau *bags*	
crys/au *shirts*	sgert/iau *skirts*	
llwy/au *spoons*	esgid/iau *shoes*	
trowsus/au *trousers*	plât>platiau *plates*	
papur/au *papers*	ffilm/iau *films*	
wy/au *eggs*	record/iau *records*	
trên//trenau *trains*	caset/iau *cassettes*	
siop/au *shops*		

102

-i
llestr/i *dishes*
siocled/i *chocolate*
tref/i *towns*
pentref/i *villages*
siaced/i *jackets*

-oedd
gwin/oedd *wines*
stryd/oedd *streets*
dinas/oedd *cities*

-iaid
anifail>anifeiliaid   *animals*

-ys *or* -s
tei/s *ties*
cês>cesys *cases*
blows/ys *blouses*

Others are more irregluar or less common:

tŷ	>tai	*houses*
car	>ceir	*cars*
coeden	>coed	*trees*
blodyn	>blodau	*flowers*
fforc	>ffyrc	*forks*
cyllell	>cyllyll	*knives*
pysgodyn	>pysgod	*fish*
bachgen	>bechgyn	*boys*
gŵr	>gwŷr	*men*
merch	>merched	*girls*
ffermwr	>ffermwyr	*farmers*

Mae Janet a Mari wedi mynd i siopa. Maen nhw yn y dre, ac maen nhw wedi edrych ar lawer o siopau. Mae Janet wedi bod yn chwilio am anrhegion.

Mari: Mae'r siop ddillad yn llawn o bethau pert! Wyt ti'n moyn prynu dillad?

Janet: Ond pa faint? Dw i ddim yn gwybod pa faint i brynu? A dw i ddim eisiau prynu pethau trwm.

Mari: Wyt ti'n moyn prynu blowsys neu sgertiau i'r merched? Beth am sanau?

Janet: Mae digon o sgertiau 'da nhw. Ac mae digon o drowsusau'da'r bechgyn. Beth yw pris y sanau?

Mari: Dwy bunt y pâr. Maen nhw'n ddrud. Beth am siacedi? Mae siacedi lliwgar yma.

Janet: Maen nhw'n cymryd gormod o le. Ond mae sgarffiaugwlân neis yma. Beth yw pris y sgarffiau?

Mari: Chwe phunt yr un. Maen nhw'n eitha rhad. Mae'r sgarffiau'n dod o ffatri wlân yn Sir Gaerfyrddin.

Janet: Iawn, rydw i'n mynd i brynu sgarff yr un i'r merched. Beth arall ydw i'n gallu prynu?

Mari: Wyt ti wedi meddwl am brynu llyfrau?

Janet: Mae llyfrau'n rhy drwm.

Mari: Beth am gasetiau a recordiau? Mae'r siop lyfrau rownd y gornel.

Janet: Syniad da.

Yn y siop lyfrau:

Mari: Mae Janet yn chwilio am casetiau neu recordiau Cymraeg i fynd nôl i America.

Siopwr: Pa fath o gerddoriaeth ydych chi'n hoffi?

Janet: Wi'n hoffi caneuon gwerin. Oes casetiau caneuon gwerin 'da chi?

Siopwr: Tapiau neu ddisgiau?

Janet: Disgiau, os gwelwch yn dda. How much are the disks?

Siopwr: Deuddeg punt yr un. Dafydd Iwan yw'r canwr mwya poblogaidd. Ydych chi wedi clywed caneuon Meic Stevens?

Janet: Ydw, rwy'n hoffi Meic Stevens - pedwar disg o ganeuon Dafydd Iwan, a thri disg o ganeuon Meic Stevens, os gwelwch yn dda.

Siopwr: Dyna wyth deg pedwar punt.

Janet: Ydych chi'n derbyn cerdyn American Express?

Janet and Mari have gone shopping. They are in the town, and they have looked at many shops. Janet has been looking for presents.

Mari:	The clothes shop is full of pretty things! Do you want to buy clothes?
Janet:	But which size? I don't know which size to buy. And I don't want to buy heavy things.
Mari:	Do you want to buy blouses or skirts for the girls? What about socks?
Janet:	They have enough skirts. And the boys have enough trousers. What is the price of the socks?
Mari:	£2 a pair. They're expensive. What about jackets? There are colorful jackets here.
Janet:	They take too much space. But there are nice woollen scarves here. What is the price of the scarves?
Mari:	£6 each. They're quite cheap. The scarves come from a woollen factory in Carmarthenshire.
Janet:	Fine, I'm going to buy a scarf each for the girls. What else can I buy?
Mari:	Have you thought about books?
Janet:	Books are too heavy.
Mari:	What about cassettes and records? The book shop is around the corner.
Janet:	Good idea.
In the book shop:	
Mari:	Janet is looking for Welsh cassettes or records to go back to America.
Shopkeeper:	What kind of music do you like?
Janet:	I like folk songs. Have you got folk songs?
Shopkeeper:	Tapes or disks?
Janet:	Disks, please. How much are the disks?
Shopkeeper:	£12 each. Dafydd Iwan is the most popular singer. Have you heard Meic Stevens' songs?
Janet:	Yes, I like Meic Stevens - four disks of Dafydd Iwan songs, and three disks of Meic Stevens' songs, please.
Shopkeeper:	That's £84.
Janet:	Do you accept an American Express card?

GEIRFA: VOCABULARY

llawn o	full of	rhy	too
peth/au (m)	thing/s	(followed by soft mutation)	
trwm	heavy	rownd	around
lliwgar	colorful	deuddeg	twelve
gwlân (m)	wool	(used with time and money)	
ffatri (f)	factory	caset/iau (m)	cassette/s
drud	expensive	record/iau (f)	record/s
rhad	cheap	tâp > tapiau (m)	tape/s
yr un	each	canwr (m)	singer
y pwys	per pound	cân > caneuon (f)	song/s
	(in weight)	disg/iau (m)	disk/s

YMARFERION: EXCERCISES

1. Use plural nouns in these sentences:
   Rwy'n prynu llyfr, caset a record.
   Mae hi wedi prynu tâp, sgert a sgarff i'r ferch.
   Maen nhw wedi prynu trowsus i'r bachgen.
2. Translate the following:
   £5 each.   £2 per pound.   £10 per pair.
3. Say that you have been shopping this morning. Say that you went to the clothes shop and the book shop. Say that you have bought a jacket, 5 books and a tape.

EXTRA GRAMMAR

'Too' with adjectives:
'Rhy' is followed by soft mutation, except for 'll' and 'rh':
Mae hi'n rhy boeth   *It is too hot*
Mae hi'n rhy ddrud   *It is too expensive*
Mae hi'n rhy rhad   *It is too cheap.*
'Quite' with adjectives:
'Eitha'
Mae e'n eitha da *it's quite good*
Maen nhw'n eitha drud *they're quite expensive*
'It'
As all nouns are feminine or masculine, 'it' must be translated either by 'e' (*he*) or by ' hi' (*she*), according to the gender of the noun:
Mae e (trowsus) yn rhad.   Mae hi (sgert) yn ddrud.

106

GWERS UN DEG DAU: YN SWYDDFA'R POST
LESSON TWELVE: AT THE POST OFFICE

stamp (m)	stamp	ail ddosbarth	second class
llythyr (m)	letter	siec (f)	check
amlen (f)	envelope	parsel (m)	parcel
cerdyn (m)	card	ffôn (m)	phone
cerdyn ffôn	phone card	ffonio	(to) telephone
postio	(to) post	talu	(to) pay
pwyso	(to) weigh	galwad ffôn (f)	phone call
post awyr	air mail	newid (m)	change
dosbarth cyntaf	first class	newid	(to) change
arian (m)	money		

GRAMADEG: GRAMMAR
Some prepositions change according to the following pronoun:
i - to
i fi *to me*; i ti *to you*; iddo fe *to him*; iddi hi *to her*; i ni *to us*; i chi *to you*; iddyn nhw *to them.*
Phrases using 'i' (*to*): the verb following 'i' is soft mutated

Mae'n	well	i fi	fynd	*It's better for me to go*
	bryd	i ti	ffonio	*It's time for you to phone*
	hen bryd	iddo fe	ddod	*It's about time he came*
	rhaid	iddi hi	aros	*She must stay*
	werth	i ni	aros	*It's worth us waiting*
	bosibl	i chi	bostio	*It's possible for you to post*
	hawdd	iddyn nhw	dalu	*It's easy for them to pay.*

ar - on
arna i *on me*; arnat ti *on you*; arno fe *on him*; arni hi *on her*; arnon ni *on us*; arnoch chi *on you*; arnyn nhw *on them.*
Phrases using 'ar' (on):

Mae dyled arna i *I am in debt*   Mae bai arna i *I am at fault*
Mae annwyd arna i *I have a cold*   Mae angen cot arna i *I need a coat*
Mae hi ar ben arna i *I'm finished*
o - of, from
ohono i *of me*; ohonot ti *of you*; ohono fe *of him*; ohoni hi *of her*; ohonon ni *of us*; ohonoch chi *of you*; ohonyn nhw *of them.*
Phrases using 'o': 'o' can be used with numbers higher than ten, followed by plural nouns: tri deg o blant *thirty children.*

Mae Janet wedi mynd i Swyddfa'r Post. Mae hi eisiau anfon cardiau post a llythyrau i America.

Janet:	Prynhawn da! Shwd ych chi?
Clerc:	Prynhawn da! Yn dda iawn diolch. Ga i helpu?
Janet:	Mae angen anfon llythyrau a chardiau i America arna i. Faint yw stamp i America?
Clerc:	Llai na 10 gram - pedwar deg tri o geiniogau. Llai na dau ddeg gram, chwe deg tri o geiniogau.
Janet:	Mae'n well i fi gael deg stamp pedwar deg tri o geiniogau, os gwelwch yn dda.
Clerc:	Dyna bedair punt, tri deg ceiniog.
Janet:	Ac mae angen postio pum llythyr arna i.
Clerc:	Mae rhaid i fi bwyso'r llythyrau. Ydy'r llythyrau 'da chi?
Janet:	Ydyn. Dyma nhw.
Clerc:	Maen nhw i gyd o dan ddau ddeg gram. Dyna dair punt a phymtheg ceiniog. Cyfanswm o saith punt, pedwar deg pum ceiniog.
Janet:	Dyma bapur deg punt.
Clerc:	A dwy bunt pum deg pum ceiniog o newid.
Janet:	Ydy hi'n bosibl i fi ffonio i America?
Clerc:	Ydy, wrth gwrs, does dim problem. Mae'r ffôn yn y gornel. Ond mae'n well i chi brynu cerdyn ffôn.
Janet:	Faint yw cerdyn ffôn?
Clerc:	Dwy bunt, pum punt neu ddeg punt.
Janet:	Un cerdyn am bum punt, os gwelwch yn dda.
Clerc:	Dyma fe.
Janet:	Mae hi'n hen bryd i fi ffonio America. Dw i ddim wedi ffonio'r plant ers wythnos. Mae bai arna i.
Clerc:	Pob hwyl.
Janet:	Pob hwyl a diolch.

Janet has gone to the Post Office. She wants to send postcards and letters to America.

Janet:	Good afternoon! How are you?
Clerk:	Good afternoon! Very well, thanks. May I help?
Janet:	I need to send letters and cards to America. How much is a stamp to America?
Clerk:	Less than 10 g - 43 pence. Less than 20g, 63 pence.
Janet:	I'd better have 10 43p stamps, please.
Clerk:	That's £4.30p.
Janet:	And I need to post five letters.
Clerk:	I have to weigh the letters. Have you got the letters?
Janet:	Yes, here they are.
Clerk:	They are all under 20g. That's £3.15p. A total of £7.45p.
Janet:	Here's a £10 note.
Clerk:	And £2.55p change.
Janet:	Is it possible for me to telephone to America?
Clerk:	Yes, of course, there's no problem. The phone is in the corner. But you'd better buy a phone card.
Janet:	How much is a phone card?
Clerk:	£2, £5 or £10.
Janet:	One card at £5, please.
Clerk:	Here it is.
Janet:	It's about time I phoned America. I haven't phoned the children for a week. I'm at fault.
Clerk:	Good bye.
Janet:	Good bye and thanks.

GEIRFA: VOCABULARY

llai na	less than	dim problem	no problem
mwy na	more than	ers	since, for
gwell na	better than	wythnos (f)	week
gwaeth na	worse than	mis (m)	month
gram (m)	gram	blwyddyn (f)	year
cyfanswm (m)	total	dydd (m)	day

YMARFERION: EXCERCISES

1.   Make up sentences using words from each of these columns:

Mae'n	rhaid	i fi	brynu	stampiau
	well	i chi	ffonio	i America
	bryd	iddo fe	anfon	'r plant
	hen bryd			llythyr
				cerdyn

2.
a)   Say you need five stamps at 43p.
b)   Say you want to telephone to America.
c)   Ask how much is a phone card.
d)   Ask where you can post letters.
e)   Say you are looking for the post office.

EXTRA GRAMMAR

1.   Note the changes in the following preposition:
at - towards, to
ata i *towards me*; atat ti *towards you*, ato fe *towards him*; ati hi *towards her*; aton ni *towards us*; atoch chi *towards you*; atyn nhw *towards them*.

2.   Note the following prepositions. All these are followed by soft mutation.

am	for, at	dros	over
gan	by, with	trwy	through
heb	without	wrth	by
dan	under	hyd	until

GWERS UN DEG TRI: YN Y CAR
LESSON THIRTEEN: IN THE CAR

petrol (m)	petrol	milltir (f)	mile
galwyn (m)	gallon	modurdy (m)	garage
olew (m)	oil	garej (f)	garage
teiar (m)	tire	gorsaf betrol (f)	petrol station
awyr (f)	air	arwydd (f/m)	sign
pwysedd (m)	pressure	dim aros	no waiting
sedd flaen (f)	front seat	ffordd fawr (f)	main road
sedd gefn (f)	back seat	map (m)	map
llogi	(to) hire	golau (m)	light
torri lawr	(to) break down	goleuadau (pl)	lights
gwasnanaethau	services	gyrrwr (m)	driver
heol (f)	road	tacsi (m)	taxi
traffordd (f)	motorway	gyrru	(to) drive
taith (f)	journey		

GRAMADEG: GRAMMAR
Past tense: imperfect: was, were
To say that something was happenning, use 'roedd' instead of 'mae':

Mae'r bws yn dod	*The bus is coming*
Roedd y bws yn dod	*The bus was coming*

Here is a full list:

Roeddwn	i'n	mynd	*I was going*
Roeddet	ti'n	gyrru	*You were driving*
Roedd	e'n	cerdded	*He was walking*
Roedd	hi'n	aros	*She was waiting*
Roedd	Sian yn	mynd	*Sian was going*
Roedd	y plant yn	chwarae	*The children were playing*
Roedden	ni'n	dod	*We were coming*
Roeddech	chi'n	cysgu	*You were sleeping*
Roedden	nhw'n	rhedeg	*They were running*

Alternative forms of the above, especially when talking:

Roeddwn i	Ro'n i	Roedden ni	Ro'n ni
Roeddet ti	Ro't ti	Roeddech chi	Ro'ch chi
Roedd e	Ro'dd e	Roedden nhw	Ro'n nhw
Roedd hi	Ro'dd hi		

To ask questions, simply drop the first 'r':

O'ch chi'n gyrru?	*Were you driving?*	O'n	*Yes*;	Na	*No*
O'dd hi'n aros?	*Was she waiting?*	O'dd	*Yes*;	Na	*No*
Oedd e'n mynd?	*Was he going?*	Oedd	*Yes*	Na	*No*

111

Mae Janet wedi llogi car am y penwythnos. Roedd hi a Mari eisiau mynd i Fangor, ond maen nhw ar goll.

Janet: Ydw i'n troi i'r chwith fan hyn?

Mari: O daro, does dim syniad 'da fi ble ry'n ni.

Janet: Ble oedden ni bore mae?

Mari: Ro'n ni yn y Bala, wrth gwrs. Wedyn ro'n ni ar y ffordd i Ffestiniog. Wedyn ro'n ni ar y ffordd i Fangor.

Janet: Ond roedd yr arwyddion yn glir. Dwyt ti ddim yn gallu darllen y map!

Mari: Ond doedd yr arwyddion ddim yn glir. Do't ti ddim yn gwybod ble i fynd chwaith.

Janet: O wel, roedd y daith yn braf.

Mari: Ac ro'n ni wedi cael bwyd da yn y Bala.

Janet: O't ti wedi cael oen?

Mari: O'n. Roedd e'n flasus iawn.

Janet: Wel, mae'n well i ni fynd i'r garej i gael petrol ac i ofyn y ffordd.

Yn y garej

Janet: Chwe galwyn o betrol. os gwelwch yn dda.

Dyn y garej: Croeso. Oes angen olew arnoch chi?

Janet: Na, mae digon o olew yn y car. Ond wi am roi awyr yn y teiars.

Dyn y garej: Dim problem. Mae'r peiriant ar y dde. Unrhyw beth arall?

Janet: Oes. Ryn ni ar goll. Beth yw'r ffordd orau i fynd i Fangor?

Dyn y garej: Dy'ch chi ddim yn bell. Trowch i'ch chwith i'r ffordd fawr, wedyn i'r dde.

Janet: Pa mor bell yw Bangor?

Dyn y garej: Ugain milltir. Ydych chi eisiau prynu map?

Janet: Na, mae map 'da ni, diolch.

Mari: Diolch byth, dy'n ni ddim wedi torri lawr.

Janet has hired a car for the weekend. She and Mari wanted to go to Bangor. But they are lost.

Janet:	Do I turn left here?
Mari:	Oh dear, I've got no idea where we are.
Janet:	Where were we this morning?
Mari:	We were in Bala. Then we were on the way to Ffestiniog. Then we were on the way to Bangor.
Janet:	But the signs were clear! You can't read the map.
Mari:	But the signs were not clear. You didn't know where to go either.
Janet:	Oh well, the journey was fine.
Mari:	And we had good food in Bala.
Janet:	Did you have lamb?
Mari:	Yes. It was very tasty.
Janet:	Well, we'd better go to the garage to have petrol and to ask the way.

In the garage

Janet:	Six gallons of petrol, please.
Garage man:	Welcome. Do you need oil?
Janet:	No, there's enough oil in the car. But I want to put air in the tires.
Garage man:	No problem. The machine is on the right. Anything else?
Janet:	Yes. We're lost. What is the best way to go to Bangor?
Garage man:	You're not far. Turn to the left to the main road, then to the right.
Janet:	How far is Bangor?
Garage man:	Twenty miles. Do you want to buy a map?
Janet:	No, we have a map, thanks.
Mari:	Thank goodness, we haven't broken down.

GEIRFA: VOCABULARY

penwythnos	weekend	clir	clear
gogledd	north	chwaith	either
de	south	blasus	tasty
ar goll	lost	peiriant	machine, engine
fan hyn	here	gorau	best
wedyn	then	pa mor bell ?	how far ?
arwyddion	signs	diolch byth	thank goodness

YMARFERION: EXCERCISES

1. Make up sentences using words from the following columns:

Ro'n	i'n	gyrru	yn y car	i Fangor
		dal	y bws	i Fethesda
		mynd	yn y trên	i Aberystwyth
		cerdded	ar y ffordd	i'r Bala
		rhedeg	ar yr heol	i Gaernarfon

2. Say where you were on holiday last year:

Ro'n i	yn	yr Almaen	*Germany*
		Ewrop	*Europe*
		yr Eidal	*Italy*
		yr Unol Daleithiau	*the USA*
		gartre	*at home*

EXTRA GRAMMAR

1.   How to say you were not: Imperfect negative:
Put 'd' instead of 'r', and insert 'ddim' after the subject:

Do'n i ddim yn gyrru	*I wasn't driving*
Do'dd e ddim yno	*He wasn't there*
Do'n ni ddim yn yfed	*We weren't drinking*
Do'n ni ddim ar goll	*We weren't lost*
Doedd Huw ddim yn cysgu	*Huw wasn't sleeping*

2.   How to say you 'had' done something: pluperfect

Simply put 'wedi' instead of 'yn':

Ro'n i wedi gyrru	*I had driven*
Do'n ni ddim wedi yfed	*We had not drunk*
Doedd Huw ddim wedi cysgu	*Huw had not slept*
Ro'n i wedi cael cinio	*I had had dinner*
O'ch chi wedi gweld y ffilm?	*Had you seen the film? / Did you see the film?*

cae (m) / caeau	field /s	coeden (f) / coed	tree /s
afon (f) /afonydd	river /s	llyn (m) / llynnoedd	lake /s
nant (m) / nentydd	brook /s	bryn (m) / bryniau	hill /s
mynydd (m) / mynyddoedd	mountain /s	gwersyll (m) / gwersylloedd	camp /s
clawdd (m) / cloddiau	hedge /s	aderyn (m) / adar	bird /s
blodyn (m) / blodau	flower /s	dafad (f) / defaid	sheep
anifail (m) / anifeiliaid	animal /s	buwch (f) / buchod	cow /s
ceffyl (m) / ceffylau	horse /s	iâr (f) / ieir	hen /s
ci (m) / cŵn	dog /s	mochyn (m) / moch	pig /s
cath (f) / cathod	cat /s	pabell (f) / pebyll	tent /s
cyw (m) / cywion	chicken /s	fferm (f) / ffermydd	farm /s

GRAMADEG: GRAMMAR

1. Commands:

When talking to more than one person, or a person you do not know well, add 'wch' to the stem of the verb (the stem is usually found by dropping off the last vowel; some verbs are more irregular). When talking to a person you know well, add 'a' to the stem of the verb:

cysgu	cysgwch	cysga	*go to sleep!*
codi	codwch	coda	*get up!*
edrych	edrychwch	edrycha	*look!*
eistedd	eisteddwch	eistedda	*sit down!*
dod	dewch	dere	*come!*
mynd	ewch	cer	*go!*
gwneud	gwnewch	gwna	*do* or *make!*

2. Possessive pronouns: my, your, his, her, our, their:

These have two elements in Welsh: the first is put before the noun, and the second after it. It is possible to use the first on its own. Some of them cause mutations,

e.g.   ci   (dog)

fy ... i	my	fy nghi i	my dog (+ nasal mutation)
dy ... di	your	dy gi di	your dog(+ soft mutation)
ei ... e	his	ei gi e	his dog (+ soft mutation)
ei ... hi	her	ei chi hi	her dog (+ aspirate mutation)
ein... ni	our	ein ci ni	our dog (no mutation)
eich ... chi	your	eich ci chi	your dog(no mutation)
eu ... nhw	their	eu ci nhw	their dog(no mutation)

Ar ôl aros ym Mangor, roedd Janet a Mari wedi mynd i Sir Fôn. Roedden nhw eisiau gwersylla.

Mari:	Edrycha! Mae'r wlad yn hyfryd. Wyt ti'n hoffi ein gwlad ni?
Janet:	Ydw, mae'r mynyddoedd a'r coed yn ogoneddus.
Mari:	Wyt ti wedi cofio dy babell di?
Janet:	Ydw, mae'r babell yn fy nghar i. Pabell fy mrawd i yw hi. Edrycha! Mae arwydd gwersyll fan'na.
Mari:	Oes. Mae'r gwersyll yn y fferm. Gyrra i mewn.
Ffermwr:	Prynhawn da! Ydych chi am wersylla fan hyn?
Mari:	Ydyn, os gwelwch yn dda.
Ffermwr:	Wel, bydd digon o gwmni i chi fan hyn: edrychwch ar fy anifeiliaid i, fy muchod i, fy moch i, fy nefaid i ... maen nhw i gyd yn aros amdanoch chi.
Mari:	Faint yw cost pabell a dau oedolyn am ddwy noson?
Ffermwr:	Pum punt am babell, dwy bunt y person: dyna naw punt y noson.
Janet:	Oes tai bach a chawod yn y gwersyll?
Ffermwr:	Oes, mae ein cyfleusterau ni wrth y ffermdy.

Yn y nos:

Mari:	Wyt ti wedi deffro? Wyt ti ar ddihun?
Janet:	Cysga, er mwyn popeth!
Mari:	Dwi i ddim yn gallu cysgu. Mae 'mhen i'n dost. Mae annwyd arna i.
Janet:	Beth yw'r sŵn yna?
Mari:	O na, yr anifeiliaid! Mae'r ffermwr yn cysgu'n hapus, ond mae ei fuchod e, ei geffylau fe, ei gathod e, ei foch e i gyd yn cadw sŵn!
Janet:	Rwy'n mynd i gwyno yn y bore.
Mari:	Rwy'n codi nawr. Dere, dere i gwyno nawr.

After staying in Bangor, Janet and Mari had gone to Anglesey. They wanted to camp.

Mari:	Look! The country is lovely. Do you like our country?
Janet:	Yes, the mountains and the trees are wonderful.
Mari:	Have you remembered your tent?
Janet:	Yes, the tent is in my car. It's my brother's tent. Look! There is a camping sign over there.
Mari:	Yes. The camp is in the farm. Drive in.
Farmer:	Good afternoon! Do you want to camp here?
Mari:	Yes, please.
Farmer:	Well, there'll be enough company for you here; look at my animals, my cows, my pigs, my sheep... they are all waiting for you.
Mari:	How much is the cost of a tent and two adults for two nights?
Farmer:	£5 for a tent, £2 per person: that is £9 per night.
Janet:	Are there toilets and a shower in the camp?
Farmer:	Yes, our facilities are by the farmhouse.

In the night:

Mari:	Have you woken up? Are you awake?
Janet:	Go to sleep, for goodness' sake.
Mari:	I can't sleep. My head is ill. I have a cold.
Janet:	What is that noise?
Mari:	Oh, no, the animals! The farmer is sleeping happily, but his cows, his horses, his cats, his pigs are all making noise!
Janet:	I'm going to complain in the morning.
Mari:	I'm getting up now. Come, come to complain now.

GEIRFA: VOCABULARY

ym Mangor	in Bangor	oedolyn (m)	adult
Sir Fôn	Anglesey	tai bach	toilets
gwersylla	(to) camp	deffro	(to) wake up
gogoneddus	wonderful	ar ddihun	awake
fan'na	over there	yn dost	ill
cwmni (m)	company	hapus	happy
brawd (m)	brother	er mwyn	for goodness'
chwaer (f)	sister	popeth	sake
tad (m)	father	i gyd	all (used
mam (f)	mother		*after* the noun)
aros am	(to) wait for	cadw sŵn	(to) make noise
		cwyno	complain

YMARFERION: EXCERCISES:

1. Put 'fy... i' around the following words (see grammar below first): tad, pentref, tref, dinas, gwlad, gwely, pabell, car, basged.

2. Make up sentences using words from the following columns (note that the 'i' has been omitted; the meaning is the same):

Mae	fy	nghath	yn	dost
		nghi		hapus
Roedd		ngheffyl		cysgu
		muwch		cadw sŵn

120

EXTRA GRAMMAR

1. **Nasal mutation. These are the changes:**

c	>	ngh	car	>	fy nghar i		*my car*
p	>	mh	pentref	>	fy mhentref i		*my village*
t	>	nh	tŷ	>	fy nhŷ		*my house*
g	>	ng	gwlad	>	fy ngwlad i		*my country*
b	>	m	basged	>	fy masged i		*my village*
d	>	n	dant	>	fy nant i		*my tooth*

2. **The nasal mutation occurs after the following:**
   a) **after 'fy' (my), as above**
   b) **after 'yn' (in), (note the various forms of 'yn'):**

Caerdydd	>	yng Nghaerdydd	*in Cardiff*
Paris	>	ym Mharis	*in Paris*
Talybont	>	yn Nhalybont	*in Talybont*
Gwent	>	yng Ngwent	*in Gwent*
Bangor	>	ym Mangor	*in Bangor*
Dinbych	>	yn Ninbych	*in Denbigh*
Cymru	>	yng Nghymru	*in Wales*

121

GWERS UN DEG PUMP: GYDA'R MEDDYG
LESSON FIFTEEN: AT THE DOCTOR'S

meddyg (m)	doctor	ceg (f)	mouth
meddygfa (f)	surgery	tafod (m)	tongue
pen tost	headache	brest (f)	chest
llygad (m) / llygaid	eye	enw cyntaf	first name
braich (f) / breichiau	arm /s	cyfenw (m)	surname
coes (f) / coesau	leg /s	cyfeiriad (m)	address
clust (f) / clustiau	ear	yswiriant (m)	insurance
llaw (f) / dwylo	hand /s	moddion (pl)	medicine
bys (m) / bysedd	finger /s	gwallt (pl)	hair
enw (m) / enwau	name /s	trwyn (m)	nose
tabled (m) / tabledi	pill, tablet	troed (f) / traed	foot / feet
papur meddyg (m)	prescription	llwnc (m)	throat

GRAMADEG: GRAMMAR

1. **Pronoun object of the verb:**
   The forms of the possessive pronoun are used as object of the verb, e.g.

   talu   *(to) pay*:

Mae e wedi	fy nhalu i	*He has*	*paid me*
	dy dalu di		*paid you*
	ei dalu e		*paid him*
	ei thalu hi		*paid her*
	ein talu ni		*paid us*
	eich talu chi		*paid you*
	eu talu nhw		*paid them*

2. **Pronouns in noun clauses:**

The noun clause (introduced by 'that' in English, e.g. I know *that* he is coming) is introduced by 'bod' in Welsh, followed by 'yn' or 'wedi' with verbs:

*I know **that the bus is coming**.*   Rwy'n gwybod **bod y bws yn dod**.
*I know **that the bus has come**.*   Rwy'n gwybod **bod y bws wedi dod**.

When used with pronouns, the same forms as the possessive pronouns are used, and are put around the word 'bod':

fy mod i	*that I am*	ein bod ni	*that we are*
dy fod ti	*that you are*	eich bod chi	*that you are*
ei fod e	*that he is*	eu bod nhw	*that they are*
ei bod hi	*that she is*		

e.g.   *I know that he is coming.*   Rwy'n gwybod ei fod e'n dod.
    I know that he has come.   Rwy'n gwybod ei fod e wedi dod.

Mae Janet yn gwybod ei bod hi'n dost.

Mari: Mae'n well i ti weld y meddyg.
Janet: Ond dw i ddim eisiau ei weld e.
Mari: Mae'n rhaid i ti. Rwy'n credu bod meddyg yn y pentref.

Maen nhw'n mynd i'r feddygfa.

Meddyg: Dewch i mewn. Beth sy'n bod arnoch chi?
Janet: Rwy'n credu bod gwres arna i. Mae peswch arna i, ac
          mae annwyd arna i, ac mae pen tost arna i.
Meddyg: Ydych chi'n credu bod ffliw arnoch chi?
Janet: Rwy'n credu ei fod e arna i, ond dw i ddim yn siŵr.
Meddyg: Mae rhaid i fi gymryd eich gwres chi. Oes, mae gwres
          arnoch chi. Rwy'n siŵr bod ffliw arnoch chi.
Janet: Beth ydw i'n gallu gwneud nawr?
Meddyg: Rydw i'n mynd i roi papur meddyg i chi. Cymerwch y
          moddion tair gwaith y dydd. Byddwch chi'n well ar ôl tri
          dydd.
Janet: Sut ydw i'n gallu'ch talu chi?
Meddyg: Oes yswiriant 'da chi?
Janet: Oes, rwy'n siŵr bod yswiriant 'da fi.
Meddyg: Wel, dyma ffurflen. Llanwch y ffurflen, os gwelwch yn
          dda.
Janet: Enw cyntaf, Janet; Cyfenw Hughes; Cyfeiriad, 1 State
          Gardens; Rhif yswiriant, un, dau, saith, pump, pedwar.
          Dyna ni.
Meddyg: Diolch yn fawr. Ewch â'r ffurflen yn ôl i America, a bydd
          yr yswiriant yn talu.
Janet: Diolch yn fawr. Wi'n mynd i aros mewn gwesty heno.
          Rwy'n credu 'mod i wedi cael hen ddigon o wersylla.

Janet knows that she is ill.

Mari: You'd better see the doctor.

Janet: But I don't want to see him.

Mari: You must. I think that there is a doctor in the village.

They go to the surgery.

Doctor: Come in. What's the matter with you?

Janet: I think that I have a temperature. I have a cough, and I
          have a cold, and I have a headache.

Doctor: Do you think that you have the flu?

Janet: I think I have it, but I'm not sure.

Doctor: I must take your temperature. Yes, you have a
          temperature. I'm sure that you have the flu.

Janet: What can I do now?

Doctor: I'm going to give you a prescription. Take the medicine
          three times a day. You'll be better after three days.

Janet: How can I pay you?

Doctor: Have you got insurance?

Janet: Yes, I'm sure that I have insurance.

Doctor: Well, here's a form. Fill the form, please.

Janet: First name, Janet; Surname, Hughes; Address, 1 State
          Gardens; Insurance number, one, two, seven, five, four.
          There we are.

Doctor: Thank you very much. Take the form back to America,
          and the insurance will pay.

Janet: Thank you very much. I'm going to stay in a hotel to
          night. I think that I've had enough of camping.

GEIRFA: VOCABULARY

ei bod hi'n	that she is	byddwch	you'll be
gwres (m)	temperature, fever	ffurflen (f)	form
ffliw (m)	flu	llanwch	fill (in)
cymryd	(to) take	rhif (m)	number
tair gwaith	three times	ewch â	take
y dydd	a day	hen ddigon	enough by far

YMARFERION: EXCERCISES

1. Put 'fy... i' (*my*) around these words, e.g. car - fy nghar i:
    tad; gwlad; cinio; pen; coes
    Put 'ei ... e' (*his*) around these words, e.g. pen - ei ben e:
    tŷ; gardd; papur; mam; tref

2. Say that you know something:
    e.g. ... that the bus is coming: Wi'n gwybod bod y bws
                                                                  yn dod
    ... that I have a cold   ... that I am ill
    ... that I am coming   ... that I am staying in a hotel
    ... that he can pay   ... that she has insurance

3. Translate these:
    I am paying her.
    The doctor sees her.
    The man has dinner and eats it.
    She asks for a glass of wine and drinks it all.

EXTRA GRAMMAR

To form the negative noun clause, insert 'ddim', e.g.

Wi'n gwybod bod y car yn dod   Wi'n gwybod bod y car ddim yn dod.
Wi'n credu ei bod hi'n talu   Wi'n credu ei bod hi ddim yn talu.

fy mod i ddim	that I'm not
dy fod ti ddim	that you're not
ei fod e ddim	that he's not
ei bod hi ddim	that she's not
bod Huw ddim	that Hugh isn't
bod y plant ddim	that the children aren't
ein bod ni ddim	that we are not
eich bod chi ddim	that you're not
eu bod nhw ddim	that they're not

GWERS UN DEG CHWECH:
LESSON SIXTEEN:

MYND I'R GÊM
GOING TO THE GAME

gêm (f)	game	nofio	(to) swim
sgôr (m/f)	score	golff (m)	golf
rygbi (m)	rugby	cae (m)	field
hoci (m)	hockey	hanner (m)	half
pêl-droed (f)	football	hanner cyntaf	first half
gôl (m/f)	goal	ail hanner	second half
ennill	(to) win	chwaraewr (m)	player
colli	(to) lose	chwaraewyr	players
tennis (m)	tennis	cyfartal	drawn

GRAMADEG: GRAMMAR

Past tense, short form: These endings are added to the verb's stem :

	I saw & gweld	*I bought &* prynu
...es i	gweles i	prynes i
...est ti	gwelest ti	prynest ti
...odd e	gwelodd e	prynodd e
...odd hi	gwelodd hi	prynodd hi
...odd Huw	gwelodd Huw	prynodd Huw
...odd y plant	gweloddy plant	prynoddy plant
...on ni	gwelon ni	prynon ni
...och chi	gweloch chi	prynoch chi
...on nhw	gwelon nhw	prynon nhw

I got up &	*I read &*
codi	darllen
codes i	darllenes i
codest ti	darllenest ti
cododd e	darllenodd e
cododd hi	darllenodd hi
cododd Huw	darllenodd Huw
cododd y plant	darllenodd y plant
codon ni	darllenon ni
codoch chi	darllenoch chi
codon nhw	darllenon nhw

'Mynd' (*to go*) 'dod (*to come*), 'cael' (*to have*) and 'gwneud' (*to do*) are irregular:

Mynd: es i, est ti, aeth e, aeth hi, aeth Huw, aeth y plant, aethon ni, aethoch chi, aethon nhw.

Dod: des i, dest ti, daeth e, daeth hi, &.

Gwneud: gwnes i, gwnest ti, gwnaeth e, gwnaeth hi, &.

Cael: ces i, cest ti, cafodd e, cafodd hi, cafodd Huw, cafodd y plant, ceson ni, cesoch chi, ceson nhw.

The object of the short form of the verb is soft mutated:

Darllenes i lyfr *I read a book*   (Darllenes i'r llyfr *I read the book*)
Prynes i docyn *I bought a ticket* (Prynes i'r tocyn *I bought the ticket*)

QUESTIONS: Simply mutate the first letter:

Brynoch chi docyn? *Did you buy a ticket?*   *Yes*: Do
Weloch chi'r gêm? *Did you see the game?*   *No*: Na *or* Naddo

129

Aeth Janet i weld gêm bêl-droed, ond dyw hi ddim yn deall y gêm.

Janet:	Ceson ni lwc: mae sedd dda 'da ni.
Mari:	Oes, fe brynes i'r tocynnau ddoe.
Janet:	Faint costion nhw?
Mari:	Fe gostion nhw wyth punt yr un.
Janet:	Weloch chi'r chwaraewr yna.
Mari:	Do.
Janet:	Beth wnaeth e?
Mari:	Sgoriodd e gôl, wrth gwrs.
Janet:	Ydy Abertawe'n chwarae'n dda?
Mari:	Ydyn. Fe enillon nhw'r wythnos ddiwethaf, ond collon nhw nos Fercher.
Janet:	Faint sgorion nhw yn yr hanner cyntaf?
Mari:	Fe sgorion nhw dri gôl.
Janet:	A faint sgoriodd Caerdydd?
Mari:	Fe sgorion nhw un gôl.
Janet:	Edrych! Fe sgoriodd un o chwaraewyr Caerydd!
Mari:	Naddo! Fe gafodd Abertawe gic rydd.
Janet:	O diar, cic rydd, cic gosb, dw i ddim yn deall y gêm.
Mari:	Paid â phoeni! Dim ond gêm yw hi!
Janet:	Fe weles i Atlanta Braves yn chwarae: rwy'n deall pêl-fas.
Mari:	Weles i mo nhw, a dw i ddim yn deall pêl-fas.
Janet:	Wel, mae pêl-fas yn gyffrous iawn. Mae un tîm yn batio, ac yn ceisio rhedeg o gwmpas y cylch, ac mae'r tîm arall yn taflu'r bêl, ac wedyn yn ceisio dal y bêl...
Mari:	Edrych! Fe sgoriodd Abertawe eto!
Janet:	O diar, fe golles i'r gôl yna.

Janet went to see a football game, but she doesn't understand the game.

Janet: We had some luck: we've got a good seat.

Mari: Yes, I bought the tickets yesterday.

Janet: How much did they cost?

Mari: They cost £8 each.

Janet: Did you see that player?

Mari: Yes.

Janet: What did he do?

Mari: He scored a goal, of course.

Janet: Is Swansea playing well?

Mari: Yes. They won last week, but they lost on Wednesday night.

Janet: How much did they score in the first half?

Mari: They scored three goals.

Janet: And how much did Cardiff score?

Mari: They scored one goal.

Janet: Look! One of Cardiff's players scored.

Mari: No! Swansea had a free kick.

Janet: O dear, free kick, penalty, I don't understand the game.

Mari: Don't worry! It's only a game!

Janet: I saw Atlanta Braves laying: I understand baseball.

Mari: I didn't see them, and I don't understand baseball.

Janet: Well, baseball is very exciting. One team bats, and tries to run around the circle, and the other team throws the ball, and then tries to catch the ball...

Mari: Look! Swansea scored again!

Janet: O dear, I missed that goal.

GEIRFA: VOCABULARY

lwc (f)	luck	cic rydd	free kick
sedd (f)	seat	cic gosb	free kick,
fe	no meaning; it		penalty
	confirms the verb,	dim ond	only
	and causes soft	pêl-fas	baseball
	mutation	cyffrous	exciting
diwethaf	last	yna	that (yma -this)
nos Fercher	Wednesday night		
batio	(to) bat	eto	again
sgorio	(to) score	colli	miss, lose
		ceisio	(to) try (to)

YMARFERION: EXCERCISES

1. Make as many sentences as possible using words from these columns:

Gweles i	Huw	yn chwarae	yn y gêm
	Abertawe		pêl-droed
	Gaerdydd	yn ennill	y gêm
		yn colli	'r gêm

2. Say you did the following things:
saw the doctor;   scored a goal;   bought a ticket;
went to the game   won the game;   lost the ticket.

EXTRA GRAMMAR

1.   Negative of past tense, short form:

a)   Insert 'ddim' after verb; Aspirate mutation of first letter of verb where possible; otherwise soft mutation:

Prynes i docyn >	Phrynes i ddim tocyn	*I didn't buy a ticket*
Gweles i gêm >	Weles i ddim gêm	*I didn't see a game*

b)   Before names of people and the definite article ('y', ' 'r'), insert 'mo' after verb:

Prynes i'r tocyn >	Phrynes i mo'r tocyn	*I didn't buy the ticket*
Gweles i'r game >	Weles i mo'r gêm	*I didn't see the game*
Gweles i Huw >	Weles i mo Huw	*I didn't see Huw*

2.   Showing possession
When two nouns follow each other, the first is usually 'owned' by the second:

cap y bachgen	*the boy's cap*;
tîm Abertawe	*Swansea's team*;
llyfr Sian	*Sian's book*.

There is no need to translate the ''s' seen in English.

plismon (m)	policeman	dwyn	(to) steal
swyddfa (f)	office	cael ei ddal	to be caught (he)
dal	(to) catch	cael ei dal	to be caught (she)
colli	(to lose)	bag llaw (m)	handbag
lleidr (m)	thief		

GRAMADEG: GRAMMAR

Use 'cael' for 'be' to express 'to be caught'. 'Cael' is followed by forms of the possessive pronoun. This is followed by the verb, mutated :   dal   *to catch*

Rwy'n	cael	fy	nal	*I am (being) caught*
Rwyt ti'n		dy	ddal	*You're (being) caught*
Mae e'n		ei	ddal	*He's (being) caught*
Mae hi'n		ei	dal	*She's (being) caught*
Mae Sian yn		ei	dal	*Sian is (being) caught*
Mae'r plant yn	cael	eu	dal	*The children are caught*
Ry'n ni'n		ein	dal	*We're (being) caught*
Ry'ch chi'n		eich	dal	*You're (being) caught*
Maen nhw'n		eu	dal	*They're (being) caught*

In the past tense, ' 'n' is replaced by 'wedi'

gweld   *to see*

Rwy	wedi	cael	fy	ngweld	*I have been seen*
Rwyt ti			dy	weld	*You've been seen*
Mae e			ei	weld	*He's been seen*
Mae hi			ei	gweld	*She's been seen*
Mae Huw			ei	weld	*Huw has been seen*
Mae'r plant			eu	gweld	*The children have been seen*
Ry'n ni			ein	gweld	*We've been seen*
Ry' ch chi			eich	gweld	*You've been seen*
Maen nhw			eu	gweld	*They've been seen*

Questions and answers follow the usual pattern:

Ydych chi wedi cael eich dal? *Have you been caught?*
Ydw *Yes*;   Na *No.*

Negative sentences also follow the usual pattern:

Dw i ddim wedi cael fy nal   *I haven't been caught*

Mae Janet wedi dal trên o Fangor i Gaerdydd. Ond collodd hi ei bag llaw ar y trên. Mae hi'n awr yn swyddfa'r heddlu.

Janet: O diar, rwy wedi colli fy arian.

Plismon: Pryd colloch chi e?

Janet: Colles i fe ar y trên.

Plismon: Sut colloch chi fe?

Janet: Mae e wedi cael ei ddwyn.

Plismon: Wedi cael ei ddwyn?

Janet: Ydy. Roedd yr arian wedi cael ei roi yn fy mag llaw.

Plismon: Ydy'r bag llaw wedi cael ei ddwyn hefyd?

Janet: Ydy, mae f'arian i wedi cael ei ddwyn, fy mag i wedi cael ei ddwyn.

Plismon: Oes unrhyw beth arall wedi cael ei ddwyn?

Janet: Oes. Roedd llawer o bethau yn y bag.

Plismon: Beth?

Janet: Roedd persawr 'da fi, allweddi - maen nhw i gyd wedi cael eu dwyn.

Plismon: Pryd oedd popeth wedi cael ei ddwyn?

Janet: Ro'n i'n cysgu yn y trên. Roedd dau fachgen bach wedi cael eu gweld yn y trên. Roedd un bachgen wedi cael ei weld yn y tŷ bach, ac roedd un bachgen wedi cael ei weld yn y coridor.

Plismon: Aha! Mae'r bag wedi cael ei ffeindio. Mae e wedi cael ei roi i ni gan y ddau fachgen. Ro'n nhw wedi ei weld e ar y llawr yn y trên.

Mae Janet yn ysgrifennu llythyr adre:

Annwyl Sion a Sian,

Rwy wedi cael amser da yng Nghymru. Mae'r tywydd wedi bod yn dda. Mae'r wlad yn hyfryd. Mae'r mynyddoedd yn brydferth, ac mae'r trefi'n ddiddorol.

Ond heddiw yn y trên roedd fy mag i wedi cael ei ddwyn, ond diolch byth, mae'r bag wedi cael ei ffeindio.

Rwy'n dod nôl i America mewn wythnos.

Cofion gorau,

Mam

Janet has caught a train from Bangor to Cardiff. But she lost her handbag on the train. She is now at the police station.

Janet: Oh dear, I've lost my money.
Policeman: When did you lose it?
Janet: I lost it on the train.
Policeman: How did you lose it?
Janet: It's been stolen.
Policeman: Been stolen?
Janet: Yes. The money had been put in my handbag.
Policeman: Has the handbag been stolen too?
Janet: Yes, my money has been stolen, my bag has been stolen.
Policeman: Has anything else been stolen?
Janet: Yes. There were many things in the bag.
Policeman: What?
Janet: I had perfume, keys - they have all been stolen.
Policeman: When had everything been stolen?
Janet: I was sleeping in the train. Two boys had been seen in the train. One boy had been seen in the toilet, and one boy had been seen in the corridor.
Policeman: Aha! The bag has been found. The bag has been given to us by two boys. They had seen it on the floor in the train.

Janet is writing a letter home:

Dear Sion and Sian,
I have had a good time in Wales. The weather has been good. The country is nice. The mountains are beautiful, and the towns are interesting.
But today in the train my bag had been stolen, but thank goodness, it has been found.
I'm coming back to America in a week
Fond regards,
Mom

GEIRFA: VOCABULARY

persawr (m)	perfume	annwyl (a)	dear
allweddi (pl)	keys	prydferth	beautiful
coridor (m)	corridor	ffeindio	(to) find
nodyn (m)	note	cofion gorau	fond regards
gan	by		

Other ways of finishing a letter:

Pob hwyl	All the best	Dymuniadau	Best wishes
Cariad mawr	Lots of love	gorau	
Yn gywir	Yours sincerely		

YMARFERION: EXCERCISES

1. Make sentences using words from the following columns:

Mae'r	bwyd	wedi	cael	ei fwyta
	gwin	yn		ei yfed
	tocyn			ei brynu
	gêm			ei chwarae
	bag			ei ddwyn
				ei ffeindio

2. Say the following in Welsh
a) The bread has been eaten   c) The film has been seen
b) The book has been read   d) The bag has been lost

EXTRA GRAMMAR

1. To say that something *had* been done, replace 'mae' by 'roedd', "rwy' by 'ro'n' etc.:

Ro'n i wedi cael fy ngweld   *I had been seen*
Ro't ti wedi cael dy ddal   *You had been caught*
Roedd e wedi cael ei fwyta   *It had been eaten*

To say *'by'* someone, use 'gan':

Mae'r bwyd wedi cael ei fwyta gan y bechgyn   *The food has been eaten by the boys*

2. Numbers - Ordinals

1st cyntaf	4th pedwerydd	7th seithfed	10th degfed
2nd ail	5th pumed	8th wythfed	100th canfed
3rd trydydd	6th chweched	9th nawfed	

All except 'cyntaf' are put before the noun:

y tîm cyntaf *the 1st team*; y trydydd tîm *the 3rd team*.

USEFUL WORDS AND PHRASES

Days of the week

dydd Llun	Monday	nos Lun	Monday night
dydd Mawrth	Tuesday	nos Fawrth	Tuesday night
dydd Mercher	Wednesday	nos Fercher	Wednsday night
dydd Iau	Thursday	nos Iau	Thursday night
dydd Gwener	Friday	nos Wener	Friday night
dydd Sadwrn	Saturday	nos Sadwrn	Saturday night
dydd Sul	Sunday	nos Sul	Sunday night

Times of day:

heddiw	today	bore yfory	tomorrow morning
yfory	tomorrow		
ddoe	yesterday	bore ddoe	yesterday morning
bore ma	this morning		
prynhawn ma	this afternoon	neithiwr	last night
heno	tonight	nos yfory	tomorrow night

Months of the year

Ionawr	January	ym mis Ionawr	in January
Chwefror	February	ym mis Chwefror	in February
Mawrth	March		
Ebrill	April		
Mai	May		
Mehefin	June		
Gorffennaf	July		
Awst	August		
Medi	September		
Hydref	October		
Tachwedd	November		
Rhagfyr	December		

Seasons

gwanwyn	spring	yn y gwanwyn	in spring
haf	summer	yn yr haf	in summer
hydref	autumn	yn yr hydref	in autumn
gaeaf	winter	yn y gaeaf	in winter

Time

un o'r gloch	1 o'clock	wyth o'r gloch	8 o'clock
dau o'r gloch	2 o'clock	naw o'r gloch	9 o'clock
tri o'r gloch	3 o'clock	deg o'r gloch	10 o'clock
pedwar o'r gloch	4 o'clock	un ar ddeg o'r gloch	
pump o'r gloch	5 o'clock		11 o'clock
chwech o'r gloch	6 o'clock	deuddeg o'r gloch	
saith o'r gloch	7 o'clock		12 o'clock

chwarter i	a quarter to (followed by soft mutation)
chwarter wedi	a quarter past
hanner awr wedi	half past
pum munud wedi	5 past
pum munud i	5 to (followed by soft mutation)
deg munud wedi	10 past
deg munud i	10 to (followed by soft mutation)
ugain munud wedi	20 past
ugain munud i	20 to (followed by soft mutation)
pum munud ar hugain wedi	25 past
pum munud ar hugain i	25 to (followed by soft mutation.)

Festivals

Dydd Calan	New year's day
Dydd Gŵyl Ddewi	St David's Day (March 1st)
y Pasg	Easter
Calan Mai	May 1st
y Sulgwyn	Whitsun (7th Sunday after Easter)
Dydd Glyndŵr	Owain Glyndŵr's Day (Sept. 16)
Calan gaeaf	Halloween
y Nadolig	Christmas
Dydd San Steffan	Boxing Day

Countries

yr Almaen	Germany	Groeg	Greece
yr Alban	Scotland	Gwlad Belg	Belgium
America	America	Lloegr	England
Ariannin	Argentina	Llydaw	Brittany
Awstralia	Australia	Norwy	Norway
Awstria	Austria	Rwsia	Russia
Cymru	Wales	Sbaen	Spain
yr Eidal	Italy	y Swistir	Switzerland
Ffrainc	France		

USEFUL PHRASES
Welsh - English

Beth yw ... yn Gymraeg?	What is ... in Welsh
Beth yw pris y ... ?	What's the price of ... ?
Ble?	Where?
Ble mae ... ?	Where is ... ?
Pryd?	When?
Faint?	How much?
Bore da	Good morning
Croeso	Welcome
Dewch i mewn	Come in
Diolch yn fawr	Thank you very much
Dyma ...	This is ...
Eisteddwch	Sit down
Esgusodwch fi	Excuse me
Faint yw ... ?	How much is ... ?
Falch i gwrdd â chi	Pleased to meet you
Ga i ... ?	May I ... ? , May I have ... ?
Ga i helpu?	May I help?
Hwyl	Good-bye
Hwyl fawr	Good-bye
Iechyd da!	Cheers! (Good health!)
i'r chwith	to the left
i'r dde	to the right
Mae hi'n braf	It's fine
Nos da	Good night
Noswaith dda	Good evening
Oes ... 'da chi?	Have you got ... ?
Os gwelwch yn dda	Please
Prynhawn da	Good afternoon
Shwmae	How are you
Siaradwch yn araf	Speak slowly
Sut da'ch chi?	How are you?
Unwaith eto	Once again
Wi'n dysgu Cymraeg	I'm learning Welsh
yn dda iawn	very well
yn syth ymlaen	straight ahead

English - Welsh

Cheers!	Good health!
Come in	Dewch i mewn
Excuse me	Esgusodwch fi
Good afternoon	Prynhawn da
Good-bye	Hwyl, Hwyl fawr
Good evening	Noswaith dda
Good morning	Bore da
Good night	Nos da
How are you?	Shwmae? Sut da'ch chi?
Have you got ... ?	Oes ... 'da chi?
Where?	Ble?
When?	Pryd?
How much?	Faint?
How much is ... ?	Faint yw ... ?
I'm learning Welsh	Wi'n dysgu Cymraeg
It's fine	Mae hi'n braf
May I ... ? , May I have ... ?	Ga i ... ?
May I help?	Ga i helpu?
Once again	Unwaith eto
Please	Os gwelwch yn dda
Pleased to meet you	Falch i gwrdd â chi
Sit down	Eisteddwch
Speak slowly	Siaradwch yn araf
straight ahead	yn syth ymlaen
Thank you very much	Diolch yn fawr
This is ...	Dyma ...
to the left	i'r chwith
to the right	i'r dde
very well	yn dda iawn
Welcome	Croeso
What's the price of the ... ?	Beth yw pris y ... ?
What is ... in Welsh	Beth yw ... yn Gymraeg?
Where is ... ?	Ble mae ... ?

143

KEY TO EXCERCISES

Lesson 1

4.   Examples:

      Ydych chi'n siarad Cymraeg?

      Ydych chi'n siarad Ffrangeg?

      Ydych chi'n siarad Saesneg?

      Ydych chi'n siarad Eidaleg?

5.   Examples:

      Ydw, tipyn bach

      Na

6.   Examples:

      Rwy'n siarad Almaeneg

      Rwy'n siarad Eidaleg

      Rwy'n deall Cymraeg

      Rwy'n siarad Saesneg

Lesson 2

4.   Examples:

      Mae hi'n bwrw glaw heno

      Bydd hi'n sych yfory

      Mae hi'n sych heddiw

      Bydd hi'n oer yfory

      Mae hi'n braf bore ma

5.   Examples:

      Ydy hi'n bwrw glaw heddiw?

      Ydy hi'n braf heddiw?

      Fydd hi'n braf yfory?

      Fydd hi'n sych yfory?

Lesson 3

4   Examples:

      Pryd mae'r trên yn cyrraedd?

      Pryd mae'r trên yn mynd?

      Pryd mae'r bws yn gadael?

5.   b) Mae'r trên yn gadael Bangor am saith o'r gloch

      c) Mae'r bws yn gadael Caerdydd am un o'r gloch

      d) Mae'r bws yn gadael Llanelli am chwech o'r gloch

      e) Mae'r trên yn mynd i Abertawe am naw o'r gloch

Lesson 4

4   Examples:
Rydw i'n hoffi nofio yn y môr
Rydw i'n hoffi gweld ffilmiau yn y sinema
Mae hi'n hoffi gweithio yn y llyfrgell
Rydyn ni'n hoffi dysgu Cymraeg yn America
Maen nhw'n hoffi byw yn Abertawe

5.   Examples:
Athrawes ydw i
Clerc ydw i
Gwraig tŷ ydw i

Lesson 5

4.   Examples:
Ydych chi'n gwybod ble mae'r llyfrgell?
Ydych chi'n gwybod ble mae'r sinema?
Ydy'r tacsi'n mynd i'r gwesty?
Ydy'r tacsi'n mynd i'r theatr?

5.   Examples:
Ydw;   Ydw; Ydy; Ydy

6.   Ewch i'r chwith
Ewch i'r dde
Ewch yn syth ymlaen
Ewch i'r stryd fawr
Ewch i'r sinema
Ewch i'r llyfrgell
Ewch i'r gwesty

7.   Examples:
Ewch yn syth ymlaen i'r gwesty. Ewch i'r chwith i'r
llyfrgell. Ewch yn syth ymlaen i'r sinema. Ewch i'r dde i'r
stryd fawr.

Lesson 6

1.   Examples:
Dw i ddim yn hoffi ffilmiau
Dw i ddim yn hoffi dramâu
Dyw hi ddim yn hoffi nofelau

2.   I like the novel, but I don't like the film
I like walking, but I don't like swimming
I like coffee, but I don't like tea
I like Beethoven, but I don't like Mozart

3. Rwy'n hoffi Schubert, ond dw i ddim yn hoffi Brahms
Rwy'n hoffi nofelau, ond dw i ddim yn hoffi dramâu
Rwy'n hoffi Vermont, ond dw i ddim yn hoffi Abertawe
Rwy'n hoffi ffilmiau James Bond, ond dw i ddim yn hoffi ffilmiau Spielberg
Rwy'n hoffi dal bws, ond dw i ddim yn hoffi cerdded.

Lesson 7

1. Mae car 'da fi
Mae llety 'da fi
Mae ystafell sengl 'da fi
Mae gwely dwbl 'da fi
Mae lle parcio 'da fi

2. Examples:
a) Oes, mae car 'da fi
b) Na, does dim cawod 'da fi yn yr ystafell wely
c) Oes, mae gwely dwbl 'da fi
d) Na, does dim gwely sengl 'da fi

3. Rwy'n chwilio am ystafell sengl
Am sawl noson?
Am un noson
Ga i ystafell ddwbl?
Oes tŷ bach 'da hi
Oes, a chawod
Ga i'r ystafell, os gwelwch yn dda?

Lesson 8

1. Ga i wydraid o win, os gwelwch yn dda?
Ga i hanner peint o gwrw, os gwelwch yn dda?
Ga i botel o ddŵr, os gwelwch yn dda?
Ga i beint o seidir, os gwelwch yn dda?
Ga i wydraid o win gwyn, os gwelwch yn dda?
Rwy'n moyn sudd afal, os gwelwch yn dda
Rwy'n moyn sudd oren, os gwelwch yn dda
Rwy'n moyn gwydraid o win coch, os gwelwch yn dda
Rwy'n moyn hanner peint o Guinness, os gwelwch yn dda

2. pum punt; dwy bunt pum deg; tair punt pum deg; saith punt; deg punt; un bunt pum deg; wyth punt; naw punt

Lesson 9

1   Beth sy i frecwast?
Ga i gwpaned o goffi du?
Rwy'n moyn bara brown, os gwelwch yn dda
Oes llaeth 'da chi?
Ga i gig moch, tost ac wy?

2.   gwin gwyn; brecwast twym; bara brown; plât glân

3.   llwy lân; ffilm dda; fforc frwnt

Lesson 10

1.   Examples
Rwy wedi bwyta tost i frecwast
Mai hi wedi yfed te i frecwast
Rwy wedi bwyta sglodion i ginio

2.   Examples:
I frecwast, rwy wedi bwyta wy a chig moch. Rwy wedi yfed te.
I ginio, rwy wedi bwyta cyw a thatws. Rwy wedi yfed coffi.

Lesson 11

1.   Rwy'n prynu llyfrau, casetiau a recordiau
Mae hi wedi prynu tapiau, sgertiau a sgarffiau i'r merched
Maen nhw wedi prynu trowsusau i'r bechgyn

2.   pum punt yr un; dwy bunt y pwys; deg punt y pâr

3.   Rwy wedi bod yn siopa'r bore ma. Rwy wedi mynd i'r siop ddillad a'r siop lyfrau. Rwy wedi prynu siaced, pum llyfr a thâp.

Lesson 12

1.   Examples
Mae'n rhaid i fi brynu stampiau
Mae'n well i chi ffonio i America
Mae'n bryd iddo fe anfon llythyr
Mae'n hen bryd i chi ffonio'r plant

2.   a) Mae angen pum stamp pedwar deg tair ceiniog arna i
b) Rwy eisiau ffonio i America.
c) Faint yw'r cerdyn ffôn?
d) Ble galla i bostio llythyrau?
e) Rwy'n chwilio am swyddfa'r post.

Lesson 13

1. Examples:
    Ro'n i'n gyrru yn y car i Fangor
    Ro'n i'n mynd yn y trên i Aberystwyth
    Ro'n i'n rhedeg ar yr heol i'r Bala
2. Examples:
    Ro'n i yn yr Almaen
    Ro'n i yn Ewrop
    Ro'n i yn yr Unol Daleithiau

Lesson 14

1. fy nhad; fy mhentref; fy nhref; fy ninas; fy ngwlad; fy ngwely; fy mhabell; fy nghar; fy masged
2. Examples:
    Mae fy nghath yn dost
    Mae fy nghi yn cysgu
    Roedd fy ngheffyl yn cadw sŵn

Lesson 15

1. fy nghar i; fy ngwlad i; fy mhen i; fy nghoes i
    ei dŷ fe; ei ardd e; ei bapur e; ei fam e; ei dref e
2. Wi'n gwybod bod annwyd arna i
    Wi'n gwybod fy mod i'n dost
    Wi'n gwybod fy mod i'n dod
    Wi'n gwybod fy mod i'n aros mewn gwesty
    Wi'n gwybod ei fod e'n gallu talu
    Wi'n gwybod bod yswiriant 'da hi
3. Wi'n ei thalu hi
    Mae'r meddyg yn ei gweld hi
    Mae'r dyn yn cael cinio ac yn ei fwyta fe
    Mae hi'n gofyn am wydraid o win ac yn ei yfed e i gyd

Lesson 16

1. Examples
    Gweles i Huw yn chwarae yn y gêm
    Gweles i Abertawe yn colli'r gêm
    Gweles i Gaerdydd yn ennill y gêm
2. Gweles i'r meddyg; Sgories i gôl; Prynes i docyn;
    Es i i'r gêm; Enilles i'r gêm; Colles i'r tocyn

Lesson 17

1.　　Examples:
　　　　Mae'r bwyd wedi cael ei fwyta
　　　　Mae'r gwin wedi cael ei yfed
　　　　Mae'r tocyn wedi cael ei brynu
　　　　Mae'r bag wedi cael ei ffeindio

2.　　a) Mae'r bara wedi cael ei fwyta
　　　　b) Mae'r llyfr wedi cael ei ddarllen
　　　　c) Mae'r ffilm wedi cael ei gweld
　　　　d) Mae'r bag wedi cael ei golli

VOCABULARY

CYMRAEG - SAESNEG
WELSH - ENGLISH

When looking for a Welsh word in a dictionary, remember that the first letter of Welsh words can change, because of the various forms of mutation.

Words which seem to begin with a vowel (a, e, i, o, u, w, y) may really start with 'g'.

These changes can occur:
Soft mutation:

c > g;	p > b;	t > d;
g > /;	b > f;	d > dd;
ll > l;	m > f;	rh > r;

Masal mutation:

c > ngh;	p > mh;	t > nh;
g > ng;	b > m;	d > n;

Aspirate mutation:

c > ch;	p > ph;	t > th.

Here is the Welsh alphapet:
A, B, C, CH, D, DD, E, F, FF, G, NG, H, I, J, L, LL, M, N, O, P, PH, R, RH, S, T, TH, U, W, Y.
Because of the combination letters which denote one sound, 'ng', for example, will be found before 'g' and not after 'n'.

These abbreviations are used:

(a)	adjective
(adv)	adverb
(f)	feminine noun
(c)	conjunction
(m)	masculine noun
(p)	pronoun
(pl)	plural
(pr)	preposition
(v)	verb

plural of noun is shown after /

A

a (c) — and
â (pr) — with
Abertawe — Swansea
Aberteifi — Cardigan
ac (c) — and
achau (pl) — family tree
aderyn /adar (m) — bird
afal /-au (m/f) — apple
afon /-ydd (f) — river
angladd /-au (m) — funeral
yr Alban (f) — Scotland
yr Almaen (f) — Germany
Almaeneg (f) — German
allwedd /-i (f) — key
am (pr) — for, at
America (f) — America
Americanes /-au (f) — American (f)
Americanwr /Americanwyr — American (m)
anifail /anifeiliaid (m) — animal
annwyd (m) — cold
annwyl (a) — dear
anrheg /-ion (f) — present
ar (pr) — on
ar ddihun (adv) — awake
ar goll (adv) — lost
ar hyd (pr) — along
araf (a) — slow
arall (a) — other
arddangosfa /arddangosfeydd (f) — exhibition
arian (a) — silver
arian (m) — money
aros (v) — wait
aros am (v) — wait for
arwydd /-ion(f/m) — sign
athrawes /-au (f) — teacher
athro /athrawon (m) — teacher
aur (a) — gold
awyr (f) — air
awyren /-nau (f) — plane

B

baban /-od (m) — baby
bach (a) — small, little
bachgen /bechgyn (m) — boy
bag /-iau (m) — bag
bag llaw (m) — handbag
bai /beiau (m) — fault
banana /-s (m) — banana
banc /-iau (m) — bank
bar /-rau (m) — bar
bara (m) — bread
basged /-i (f) — basket
beic /-iau (m) — bicycle
berwi (v) — boil
beth? — what?
bil /-iau (m) — bill
bisgïen / bisgedi (f) — biscuit
blasus (a) — tasty
ble? — where?
ble mae? — where is?
blodyn /blodau (m) — flower
blows /-ys (f) — blouse
blwyddyn /blynyddoedd (f) — year
blynedd (pl) — years
bod (pr) — that
bod (v) — be
bore /-au (m) — morning
bowlen /-ni (f) — bowl
braf (a) — fine
braich /breichiau (f) — arm

brawd /brodyr (m)	brother
brecwast /-au (m)	breakfast
brest (f)	chest
bresychen /bresych (f)	cabbage
brithyll /-od (m)	trout
bronglwm (m)	bra
brown (a)	brown
brwnt (a)	dirty
brwsh /-ys (m)	brush
bryn /-iau (m)	hill
buwch /buchod (f)	cow
bwrdd /byrddau (m)	table
bwrw eira (v)	snow
bwrw glaw (v)	rain
bws /bysus (m)	bus
bwyd /-ydd (m)	food
bwydlen /-ni (f)	menu
bwyta (v)	eat
byd (m)	world
bydd (v)	will
bys /-edd (m)	finger

C

cadair /cadeiriau (f)	chair
cadw (v)	keep
cadw sŵn (v)	make noise
cae /-au (m)	field
cael (v)	have
Caer	Chester
Caerdydd	Cardiff
Caerfyrddin	Carmarthen
caffe /-s (m)	café
calendr /-au (m)	calendar
calon /-au (f)	heart
camera /camerâu (m)	camera

cân /caneuon (f)	song
canol (m)	center
canolfan hamdden (f)	leisure center
cant	hundred
canwr /cantorion (m)	singer
car /ceir (m)	car
cariad /-on (m)	love, sweetheart
carped /-i (m)	carpet
caru (v)	love
casét /casetiau (m)	cassette
cath /-od (f)	cat
cawod /-ydd (f)	shower
caws (m)	cheese
ceffyl /-au (m)	horse
cefn /-au (m)	back
cefnder /-oedd (m)	cousin
ceg /-au (f)	mouth
cenedl /cenhedloedd (f)	nation
cerdded (v)	walk
cerddorfa /cerddorfeydd (f)	orchestra
cerdyn /cardiau (m)	card
cês /cesys (m)	case
ci /cŵn (m)	dog
cic /-iau (f)	kick
cic gosb (f)	penalty, free kick
cic rydd (f)	free kick
cig /-oedd (m)	meat
cig moch (m)	bacon
cinio /ciniawau (m/f)	lunch, dinner

clawdd /cloddiau (m)	hedge
clerc /-od (m)	clerk
clir (a)	clear
cloc /-iau (m)	clock
clust /-iau (f)	ear
coch (a)	red
codi (v)	get up, raise, pick up
coeden /coed (f)	tree
coes /-au (f)	leg
cofion gorau	fond regards
coffi (m)	coffee
coleg /-au (m)	college
colli (v)	lose
côr /corau (m)	choir
coridor /-au (m)	corridor
cost /-au (f)	cost
crap (f)	smattering
creision (pl)	crisps
croeso (m)	welcome
crys /-au (m)	shirt
cul (a)	narrow
cwmni (m)	company
cŵn (pl)	dogs
cwpan /-au (m/f)	cup
cwpaned (m)	cupful
cwrdd â (v)	meet
cwrw (m)	beer
cwstard (m)	custard
cwyno (v)	complain
cyfanswm (m)	total
cyfeiriad /-au (m)	address
cyfenw /-au (m)	surname
cyfnither /-oedd (f)	cousin
cylchfan /-nau (f)	roundabout
cyllell /cyllyll (f)	knife
cymdeithasol (a)	social
Cymraeg (f)	Welsh
Cymreig (a)	Welsh
Cymraes (f)	Welshwoman
Cymro /Cymry (m)	Welshman
Cymru (f)	Wales
cymryd (v)	take
cymylog (a)	cloudy
cyngerdd /cyngherddau (f/m)	concert
cynnwys (v)	include
cyntaf (a)	first
cyrraedd (v)	arrive
cyw /-ion (m)	chicken

CH

chi (p)	you
chithau (p)	you (too)
chwaer /chwiorydd (f)	sister
chwaith (adv)	either
chwarae (v)	play
chwaraewr /chwaraewyr (m)	player
chwe(ch)	six
chwilio (v)	look for, search
chwith	left

D

da (a)	good
dafad /defaid (f)	sheep
dal (v)	catch
dan (pr)	under
dant /dannedd (m)	tooth
darlithydd /darlithwyr (m)	lecturer
darlun /-iau (m)	picture
darllen (v)	read
daro!	dear!
dau	two
de (m)	south
deall (v)	understand

153

dechrau (v)	start
deffro (v)	wake up
deg	ten
dere!	come!
desg /-iau (f)	desk
dewch (v)	come
dewis (v)	choose
dewis /-iadau (m)	choice
di-waith (a)	unemployed
dillad (pl)	clothes
dim (m)	nothing
dim aros	no waiting
dinas /-oedd (f)	city
Dinbych	Denbigh
diod /-ydd (f)	drink
diolch (m)	thanks
diolch byth	thank goodness
disg /-iau (m)	disk
diwedd (m)	end
diwethaf (a)	last
dod (v)	come
dosbarth /-iadau (m)	class
drama /dramâu (f)	drama
dros (pr)	over
drud (a)	expensive
du (a)	black
dwbl (a)	double
dŵr (m)	water
dwy	two
dwyn	steal
dychwel (v)	verb
dydd /-iau (m)	day
dyma	here is, here are
dyn /-ion (m)	man
dysgu (v)	learn, teach

DD

dde (adv)	right
ddoe (adv)	yesterday

E

edrych (v)	look
eglwys /-i (f)	church
ei (p)	her, his
eich (p)	your
Eidaleg (f)	Italian
eidion (m)	beef
ein (p)	our
eirin gwlanog (pl)	peaches
eirinen /eirin (f)	plum
eisiau (m, v)	want
eistedd (v)	sit
eliffant /-od (m)	elephant
ennill (v)	win
enw /-au (m)	name
enw cyntaf (m)	first name
eog /-iaid (m)	salmon
er mwyn popeth	for goodness' sake
ers (pr)	since, for
esgid /-iau (f)	shoe
esusodwch fi	excuse me
eto (adv)	again, yet
eu (p)	their

F

fan'na (adv)	over there
fe	confirms the verb
fi (p)	me
fy (p)	my
fydd (c)	will ?

FF

ffatri /ffatrioedd (f)	factory
ffeindio (v)	find

ffenestr /-i (f)	window	golau /goleuadau (m)	light
fferm /-ydd (f)	farm	golff (m)	golf
ffermwr /ffermwyr (m)	farmer	gormod (adv)	too much
ffilm /-iau (f)	film	gorsaf /-oedd (f)	station
ffliw (m)	flu	gorsaf betrol (f)	petrol station
ffôn /ffonau (m)	phone	gram /-au (m)	gram
ffonio (v)	phone	grawnwin (pl)	grapes
fforc /ffyrc (f)	fork	gwaith (m)	work
ffordd /ffyrdd (f)	way	gwallt (pl)	hair
ffordd fawr (f)	main road	gwasanaethau (pl)	services
ffowlyn /ffowls (m)	chicken	gwefus /-au (f)	lip
		gweithio (v)	work
Ffrangeg (f)	French	gweithiwr /gweithwyr (m)	worker
Ffrainc (f)	France		
ffresh (a)	fresh	gweld (v)	see
ffrio (v)	fry	gwell (a)	better
ffrog /-iau (f)	frock	gwely /-au (m)	bed
ffrwythau (pl)	fruit	gwersyll /-oedd (m)	camp
ffurflen /-ni (f)	form		
G		gwersylla (v)	camp
ga i (v)	may I have	gwerth (m)	value
gadael (v)	leave	gwerthu (v)	sell
galw (v)	call	gwesty /gwestai (m)	hotel
galwad /-au (f)	call		
galwyn /-i (m)	gallon	gwin /-oedd (m)	wine
gallu (v)	be able to	gwlad /gwledydd (f)	country
gan (pr)	by		
gardd /gerddi (f)	garden	gwlân (m)	wool
garej /-ys (f)	garage	gwneud (v)	do, make
gellygen /gellyg (f)	pear	gwraig tŷ /gwragedd tŷ (f)	housewife
		gwres (m)	fever
gêm /gemau (f)	game	gwybod (v)	know
glas (a)	blue	gwybodaeth (f)	information
gofyn (v)	ask	gwydraid (m)	glassful
gogledd (m)	north	gwyliau (pl)	holidays
gogoneddus (a)	wonderful	gwyn (a)	white
gôl /-iau (f/m)	goal	gwyrdd (a)	green
golau (a)	light	gyda (pr)	with

gyrru (v)	drive	i gyd (adv)	all
gyrrwr /gyrwyr (m)	driver	iâ (m)	ice
		iâr /ieir (f)	hen
H		iawn (a)	very, fine
halen (m)	salt	ie	yes
ham (m)	ham	iechyd da	good health, cheers
hanner /haneri (m)	half	inc /-iau (m)	ink
hapus (a)	happy	**J**	
haul /heuliau (m)	sun	jam /-iau (m)	jam
hawdd (a)	easy	jin (m)	gin
haws (a)	easier	jîns (m)	jeans
heb (pr)	without	jwg /jygiau (m)	jug
heddiw (adv)	today	**L**	
heddlu /-oedd (m)	police force	lamp /-au (f)	lamp
		lemwn /-au (m)	lemon
heddwch (m)	peace	letys (m)	lettuce
helo	hello	lifft /-iau (m)	lift
hen (a)	old	lili /lilïau (f)	lilly
hen ddigon	enough by far	lôn /lonau (f)	lane
heno (adv)	tonight	lwc (f)	luck
heol /-ydd (f)	road	**LL**	
heulog (a)	sunny	llaeth (m)	milk
hi (p)	she, her	llai (a)	less, smaller
hir (a)	long	llaw /dwylo (f)	hand
hoff (a)	fond, favorite	llawer (adv)	a lot
hoffi (v)	like	llawn (a)	full
hosan /sanau (f)	sock, stocking	lle /-fydd (m)	place
hufen iâ (m)	ice cream	lleden (f)	plaice fish
hwn (p,a)	this	lleidr /lladron (m)	thief
hwyl	good-bye	lleol (a)	local
hwyl fawr	good-bye	llestri (pl)	dishes
hy (a)	bold	llety /lletyau (m)	lodging
hyd (pr)	until	Lloegr (f)	England
hyfryd (a)	pleasant, lovely	llogi (v)	hire
		llong /-au (f)	ship
hyn (p,a)	this, these	llwnc (m)	throat
hynt (f)	story, journey	llwy /-au (f)	spoon
I		llwyd (a)	grey
i (pr)	to	llyfr /-au (m)	book

llyfrgell /-oedd (f) library
llyfrgellydd /-ion (m) librarian
llygad /llygaid (m) eye
llyn /-noedd (m) lake
llysiau (pl) vegetables
llythyr /-au (m) letter (message)
llythyren /llythrennau (f) letter (of alphabet)

M

'ma (a) this
mae (v) there is, is
mam /-au (f) mother
mam-gu /mamau cu (f) grandmother
map /-iau (m) map
marmalêd (m) marmalade
mat /-iau (m) mat
mawr (a) big
meddyg /-on (m) doctor
meddygfa /meddygfeydd (f) surgery
mêl (m) honey
melyn (a) yellow
menyn (m) butter
melys (a) sweet
menyw /-od (f) woman
merch /-ed (f) girl
mil thousand
min (m) edge
mis /-oedd (m) month
mlynedd (pl) [blynedd] years
mochyn /moch (m) pig
moddion (pl) medicine
Môn Anglesey
môr /moroedd (m) sea

moron (pl) carrots
moyn (v) want
munud /-au (m/f) minute
mwy (a) more, bigger
mwyaf (a) most, biggest
mwyn (a) mild, gentle
myfyriwr /myfyrwyr (m) student
mynd (v) go
mynydd /-oedd (m) mountain

N

na no
na (c) than
nabod (v) know
nain /neiniau (f) grandmother
nant /nentydd (m) brook
naw nine
nawfed (a) ninth
neu (c) or
neuadd /-au (f) hall
neuadd y dref (f) town hall
newid (m) change
newid (v) change
newydd (a) new
newyddion (pl) news
nhw (p) they, them
ni (p) we, us
nicyrs (m) knickers
nodyn /nodiadau (m) note
nofel /-au (f) novel
nofio (v) swim
nonsens (m) nonsense
nos /-au (f) night
noson (f) night
noswaith /nosweithiau (f) evening
nyrs /-ys (f) nurse

O

o gwmpas (pr) — around
oedolyn /oedolion (m) — adult
oen /wyn (m) — lamb
oer (a) — cold
oes (v) — is there?, yes
olew (m) — oil
oren (a) — orange
oren /-nau (m) — orange

P

pa — which
pabell /pebyll (f) — tent
pac /-iau (m) — pack
pacio (v) — pack
palas /-au (m) — palace
papur /-au (m) — paper
papur tŷ bach (m) — toilet paper
pâr /parau (m) — pair
parc /-iau (m) — park
parcio (v) — park
parsel /-i (m) — parcel
pas /-ys (f) — pass
pedwar — four
peint /-iau (m) — pint
peiriant /peiriannau (m) — machine, engine
pêl-droed (f) — football
pêl-fas (f) — baseball
pell (a) — far
pen tost (m) — headache
pensiynwr /pensiynwyr (m) — pensioner
pentref /-i (m) — village
penwythnos /-au (m) — weekend
perfformio (v) — perform
persawr (m) — perfume
pert (a) — pretty
peth /-au (m) — thing

petrol (m) — petrol, gasoline
pin /-nau (m) — pin
pinc (a) — pink
plant (pl) — children
plât /platiau (m) — plate
platfform /-au (m) — platform
plentyn /plant (m) — child
plismon /plismyn (m) — policeman
pob — every
poeni (v) — worry
popeth (m) — everything
porc (m) — pork
porffor (a) — purple
post (m) — post
postio (v) — post
pot /-iau (m) — pot
potel /-i (f) — bottle
prifysgol /-ion (f) — university
pris /-iau (m) — price
problem /-au (f) — problem
pryd (m) — time
pryd? — when?
prydferth (a) — beautiful
prynhawn /-au (m) — afternoon
prynu (v) — buy
pum(p) — five
punt /punnoedd (f) — pound (£)
pupur (m) — pepper
pur (a) — pure
pwdin /-au (m) — pudding, sweet
pwll /pyllau (m) — pit
pwll nofio (m) — swimming pool
pwys /-au (m) — pound (lb)

158

pwys o	a pound of	sawl (a)	several
pwysedd (m)	pressure	saws (m)	sauce
pwyso (v)	weigh	Sbaen (f)	Spain
pys (pl)	peas	Sbaeneg (f)	Spanish
pysgodyn /pysgod (m)	fish	swn (m)	noise
		swyddfa /swyddfeydd (f)	office

R

'r	the
radio (m)	radio
râs /rasys	race
record /-iau (f)	record
reis (m)	rice
rownd /-iau (f)	round
rownd (pr)	around
Rwsia (f)	Russia
Rwsieg (f)	Russian
rygbi (b)	rugby

RH

rhad (a)	cheap
rhaff /-au (f)	rope
rhaid (m)	must
rhedeg (v)	run
rheolwr /rheolwyr (m)	manager
rhif /-au (m)	number
rholyn /rholiau (m)	roll
rhostio (v)	roast
rhy (a)	too
rhyfel /-oedd (m)	war

S

Saesneg (f)	English
Saesnes /-au (f)	English woman
Sais /Saeson (m)	Englishman
saith	seven
salad /-au (m)	salad
sanau (pl)	socks, stockings
sawl	how many

sebon /-au (m)	soap
sedd /-au (f)	seat
sedd flaen (f)	front seat
sedd gefn (f)	back seat
sefyll (v)	stand
selsigen /selsig (f)	sausages
sengl (a)	single
seren /sêr (f)	star
sewin (m)	sewin fish
sgarff /-au (f)	scarf
sgert /-iau (f)	skirt
sglodion (pl)	chips
sgorio (v)	score
sgrîn /sgrinau (f)	screen
shwmae	how are you
siaced /-i (f)	jacket
siarad (v)	speak
siec /-iau (f)	check
sieri (m)	sherry
silff /-oedd (f)	shelf
sinema /sinemâu (m/f)	cinema
siocled /-i (m)	chocolate
siop /-au (f)	shop
siopwr /siopwyr (m)	shopkeeper, shopper
Sir Fôn (f)	Anglesey
siwgr (m)	sugar
siŵr (a)	sure
siwt /-iau (f)	suit
soser /-i (f)	saucer
stamp /-iau (m)	stamp
stryd /-oedd (f)	street

159

sudd /-oedd (m)	juice	tipyn bach	a little
sur (a)	sour	tocyn /-nau (m)	ticket
sut?	how?	tomato /-s (m)	tomato
sut'dach chi?	how are you?	ton /-nau (f)	wave
swper /-au (m)	supper	tonic (m)	tonic
swydd /-i (f)	job	torri (v)	break
swyddfa	office	torri lawr (v)	break down
/swyddfeydd		tost (m)	toast
swyddfa'r post (f)	post office	traffig (m)	traffic
sych (a)	dry	traffordd	motorway
symffoni	symphony	/traffyrdd (f)	
/symffonïau (m)		traphont /ydd (f)	viaduct
syth (a)	straight	tref /-i (f)	town
		trên /trenau (m)	train

T

tabled /-i (f)	pill	tri	three
tacsi /-s (m)	taxi	troed /traed (f)	foot
tad /-au (m)	father	trons /-au (m)	underpants
tad-cu	grandfather	trowsus /-au (m)	trousers
/tadau cu (m)		trwm (a)	heavy
taid /teidiau (m)	grandfather	trwy (pr)	through
tafarn (f)	pub	trwyn /-au (m)	nose
taflu (v)	throw	trydanwr	electrician
tafod /-au (m)	tongue	/trydanwyr (m)	
tair	three	tun /-iau (m)	tin
talu (v)	pay	twym (a)	warm, hot
tân /tanau (m)	fire	tŷ /tai (m)	house
tarten (f)	tart, pie	tŷ bach (m)	toilet
tatws (pl)	potatoes	tŷ bwyta (m)	restaurant
te (m)	tea	Tŷ Ddewi	St David's
tebot /-au (m)	teapot	tyn (a)	tight
technegydd	technician	tywel /-ion (m)	towel
/technegwyr		tywydd (m)	weather
tei /-s (m)	tie	tywyll (a)	dark

U

teiar /-s (m)	tire
teledu	television
/setiau teledu (m)	
theatr /-au (f)	theater
ti (p)	you
tic /-iau (m)	tick
ticio	(to) tick

un	one
Unol Daleithiau America	U.S.A.
unrhyw (a)	any
unwaith (adv)	once

W

wedi	has, have, after
wedyn (adv)	then, afterwards
winc (f)	wink
wrth (pr)	by, near
wrth gwrs	of course
wy /-au (m)	egg
wyth	eight
wythnos /-au (f)	week

Y

y	the
ydw	yes
ydych (v)	are, do
yfed (v)	drink
yfory (adv)	tomorrow
yma (a)	this
yma (adv)	here
ymlaen (adv)	ahead, on
yn	part of verb 'mae'
yn (pr)	in
yr	the
yr un (adv)	each
ysbyty /ysbytai(m)	hospital
ysgafn (a)	light (in weight)
ysgol /-ion (f)	school
ysgrifennu	(to) write
ysgrifenyddes /-au (f)	secretary
ystafell /-oedd (f)	room
ystafell fwyta (f)	dining room
ystafell wely (f)	bedroom
ystafell ymolchi(f)	bathroom
yswiriant (m)	insurance

SAESNEG - CYMRAEG
ENGLISH - WELSH

A

able	gallu (v), galluog (a)
address	cyfeiriad (m)
adult	oedolyn
after	wedi
afternoon	prynhawn
afterwards	wedyn
again	eto
ahead	ymlaen
air	awyr
all	i gyd
along	ar hyd
America	America
American	Americanes (f), Americanwr (m)
and	a, ac
Anglesey	Môn
animal	anifail
any	unrhyw
apple	afal
arm	braich
around	o gwmpas
arrive	cyrraedd
ask	gofyn
at	i, at
awake	ar ddihun

B

baby	baban
back	cefn (m)
back seat	sedd gefn
bacon	cig moch
bag	bag
banana	banana
bank	banc
bar	bar (m)
basket	basged
bathroom	ystafell ymolchi
beautiful	prydferth
bed	gwely
bedroom	ystafell wely
beef	cig eidion
beer	cwrw
better	gwell
bicycle	beic
big	mawr
bigger	mwy
bill	bil
bird	aderyn
biscuit	bisgïen
black	du
blouse	blows
blue	glas
boil	berwi
bold	hy
book	llyfr
bottle	potel
bowl	bowlen
boy	bachgen
bra	bronglwm
bread	bara
break	torri
break down	torri lawr
breakfast	brecwast
brook	nant
brother	brawd
brown	brown
brush	brwsh (m)
bus	bws
butter	menyn
buy	prynu
by	wrth (near), gan

C

cabbage	bresychen
café	caffe
calendar	calendr
call	galw (v), galwad (f)
camera	camera
camp	gwersyll (m), gwersylla (v)
car	car
card	cerdyn
Cardiff	Caerdydd
Cardigan	Aberteifi
Carmarthen	Caerfyrddin
carpet	carped
carrots	moron
case	cês
cassette	casét
cat	cath
catch	dal
ceg	mouth
cerdded	walk
chair	cadair
change	newid (m, v)
cheap	rhad
cheers!	iechyd da!
cheese	caws
check	siec
chest	brest
Chester	Caer
chicken	cyw, ffowlyn
child	plentyn
children	plant
chips	sglodion
chocolate	siocled
choice	dewis
choir	côr
choose	dewis
church	eglwys
cinema	sinema
city	dinas
class	dosbarth
clear	clir (a), clirio (v)
clerk	clerc
clock	cloc
clothes	dillad
cloudy	cymylog
coffee	coffi
cold	oer (a), annwyd (m)
college	coleg
come	dod
come!	dewch!, dere!
company	cwmni
complain	cwyno
concert	cyngerdd
country	gwlad
cousin	cefnder (m), cyfnither (f)
cow	buwch
crisps	creision
cup	cwpan
cupful	cwpaned
custard	cwstard

D

dark	tywyll
day	dydd
dear	annwyl (a)
dear!	daro!
Denbigh	Dinbych
desk	desg
dining room	ystafell fwyta
dinner	cinio
dirty	brwnt (a)
dishes	llestri
disk	disg
do	gwneud
doctor	meddyg

dog	ci	favourite	hoff
dogs	cŵn	fever	gwres
drama	drama	field	cae
drink	yfed (v),	film	ffilm
	diod (f)	fine	braf (a)
drive	gyrru (v)	fine	iawn (*all*
driver	gyrrwr		*right*)
dry	sych	finger	bys
E		fire	tân
each	yr un	first	cyntaf
ear	clust	first name	enw cyntaf
easier	haws	fish	pysgodyn
easy	hawdd	flower	blodyn
eat	bwyta	flu	ffliw
edge	ymyl	fond	hoff
egg	wy	food	bwyd
eight	wyth	foot	troed
either	chwaith	football	pêl-droed
electrician	trydanwr	for	am, i(*to*),
elephant	eliffant		ers(*since*)
end	diwedd	for goodness'	er mwyn
engine	peiriant	sake	popeth
England	Lloegr	fork	fforc
English	Saesneg	form	ffurflen
evening	noson	four	pedwar (m),
every	pob		pedair (f)
everything	popeth	French	Ffrangeg
excuse me	esgusodwch fi	fresh	ffresh
exhibition	arddangosfa	frock	ffrog
expensive	drud	front seat	sedd flaen
eye	llygad	fruit	ffrwythau
F		fry	ffrio
factory	ffatri	full	llawn
family tree	achau	funeral	angladd
far	pell	**G**	
farm	fferm	gallon	galwyn
farmer	ffermwr	game	gêm
father	tad	garage	garej,
fault	bai		modurdy
		garden	gardd

gasoline	petrol	her	hi, ei
gentle	mwyn		(*posession*)
German	Almaeneg	here	yma
Germany	yr Almaen	here is, here are	dyma
get up	codi	hill	bryn
gin	jin	him	fe, e
girl	merch	hire	llogi
glassful	gwydraid	his	ei
go	mynd	holidays	gwyliau
goal	gôl	honey	mêl
gold	aur	horse	ceffyl
golf	golff	hospital	ysbyty
good	da	hot	twym, poeth
good-bye	hwyl,	hotel	gwesty
	hwyl fawr	house	tŷ
gram	gram	housewife	gwraig tŷ
grandfather	tad-cu, taid	how are you?	shwd ych chi?,
grandmother	mam-gu, nain		sut 'dach chi?
grapes	grawnwin	how many	sawl
green	gwyrdd	how?	sut?
grey	llwyd	hundred	cant

H

I

hair	gwallt	ice	iâ
half	hanner	ice cream	hufen iâ
hall	neuadd	in	yn
ham	ham	include	cynnwys
hand	llaw	information	gwybodaeth
handbag	bag llaw	ink	inc
happy	hapus	insurance	yswiriant
has	wedi	is there?	oes?
have	cael	Italian	Eidaleg
have	wedi		

J

he	fe, e	jacket	siaced
headeache	pen tost	jam	jam
heart	calon	jeans	jîns
heavy	trwm	job	swydd
hedge	clawdd	journey	taith
hello	helo,	jug	jwg
	shwmae	juice	sudd
hen	iâr		

K

keep	cadw
key	allwedd
kick	cic
knickers	nicyrs
knife	cyllell
know	gwybod
know	gwybod, nabod (*a person*)

L

lake	llyn
lamb	oen
lamp	lamp
lane	lôn
last	diwethaf
learn	dysgu
leave	gadael
lecturer	darlithydd
left	chwith
leg	coes
leisure center	canolfan hamdden
lemon	lemwn
less	llai
letter (message)	llythyr
letter (of alphabet)	llythyren
lettuce	letys
librarian	llyfrgellydd
library	llyfrgell
lift	lifft
light	ysgafn (*weight*), golau (*bulb*)
like	hoffi (v), fel (c)
lilly	lili
lip	gwefus

little	bach
little, a	tipyn bach
local	lleol
lodging	llety
long	hir
look	edrych
look for	chwilio am
lose	colli
lost	ar goll
lot	llawer
love	caru (v) cariad (m)
lovely	hyfryd
luck	lwc
lunch	cinio

M

machine	peiriant
main road	ffordd fawr
make	gwneud
make o noise	cadw sŵn
man	dyn
manager	rheolwr
map	map
marmalade	marmalêd
mat	mat
may I, may I have	ga i
me	fi
meat	cig
medicine	moddion
meet	cwrdd â
menu	bwydlen
mild	mwyn
milk	llaeth, llefrith
minute	munud
money	arian
month	mis
more	mwy
morning	bore
mother	mam
motorway	traffordd

mountain	mynydd	**P**	
must	rhaid	pack	pac
my	fy	pair	pâr
N		palace	palas
name	enw (m)	paper	papur
narrow	cul	parcel	parsel
nation	cenedl	park	parc (m),
near	wrth (pr),		parcio (v)
	agos (a)	pass	pas (m),
new	newydd		pasio (v)
news	newyddion	pay	talu
night	nos, noson	peace	heddwch
	(*evening*)	peaches	eirin gwlanog
nine	naw	pear	gellygen
ninth	nawfed	peas	pys
no	na	penalty	cosb, cic gosb
noise	sŵn	pensioner	pensiynwr
nonsense	nonsens	pepper	pupur
north	gogledd	perform	perfformio
nose	trwyn	petrol	petrol
note	nodyn (m)	petrol station	gorsaf betrol
nothing	dim byd	phone	ffôn (m),
novel	nofel		ffonio (v)
number	rhif	pick up	codi
nurse	nurse	picture	darlun, llun
O		pie	tarten
of course	wrth gwrs	pig	mochyn
office	swyddfa	pill	tabled
oil	olew	pin	pin
old	hen	pink	pinc
on	ar	pint	peint
once	unwaith	pit	pwll
one	un	place	lle
or	neu	plaice fish	lleden
orange	oren (a, m)	plane	awyren
orchestra	cerddorfa	plate	plât
other	arall	platform	platfform
our	ein	play	chwarae (v),
over	dros (pr)		drama (f)
over there	fan'na	player	chwaraewr

pleasant	hyfryd	room	ystafell
plum	eirinen	rope	rhaff
police force	heddlu	round	rownd
policeman	plismon	roundabout	cylchfan
pork	porc	rugby	rygbi
post	post (m),	run	rhedeg
	postio (v)	Russia	Rwsia
post office	swyddfa'r	Russian	Rwsieg (f)
post		**S**	
pot	pot	salad	salad
potatoes	tatws	salmon	eog
pound	punt (£),	salt	halen
	pwys (lb)	sauce	saws
present	anrheg (f),	saucer	soser
	presennol (a)	sausages	selsig
pressure	pwysedd	scarf	sgarff
pretty	pert	school	ysgol
price	pris	score	sgôr
problem	problem	Scotland	yr Alban
pub	tafarn	screen	sgrîn
pudding	pwdin	sea	môr
pure	pur	search	chwilio
purple	porffor	seat	sedd
R		secretary	ysgrifenyddes
race	râs		(f)
radio	radio	see	gweld
rain	glaw (m),	sell	gwerthu
	bwrw glaw (v)	services	gwasanaethau
raise	codi	seven	saith
read	darllen	several	sawl
record	record	sewin	sewin
red	coch	she	hi
restaurant	bwyty	sheep	dafad
return	dychwel	shelf	silff
rice	reis	sherry	sieri
right	dde	ship	llong
river	afon	shirt	crys
road	heol	shoe	esgid
roast	rhostio	shop	siop
roll	rholyn (m)	shopkeeper	siopwr

shower	cawod	sun	haul
silver	arian	sunny	heulog
since	ers	supper	swper
singer	canwr	sure	siŵr
single	sengl	surname	cyfenw
sister	chwaer	Swansea	Abertawe
sit	eistedd	sweet	pwdin (m),
six	chwe(ch)		melys (a)
skirt	sgert	sweetheart	cariad (m,f)
slow	araf	swim	nofio
small	bach	swimming pool	pwll nofio
smaller	llai	symphony	symffoni
snow	eira (m),	**T**	
	bwrw eira (v)	table	bwrdd
soap	sebon	take	mynd â,
social	cymdeithasol		cymryd
sock	hosan	tart	tarten
socks	sanau	tasty	blasus
song	cân	taxi	tacsi
sour	sur	tea	te
south	de	teach	dysgu
Spanish	Sbaeneg	teacher	athrawes (f),
speak	siarad		athro (m)
spoon	llwy	technician	technegydd
St Davids	Tŷ Ddewi	television	teledu
stamp	stamp	ten	deg
stand	sefyll (v)	tent	pabell
star	seren	than	na
start	dechrau	thank goodness	diolch byth
station	gorsaf	thanks	diolch
steal	dwyn	that	bod (pr, v)
stocking	hosan	the	y, yr, 'r
stockings	sanau	theater	theatr
story	stori	their	eu
straight	syth	them	nhw
straight ahead	yn syth ymlaen	then	wedyn
street	stryd	there is, there are	mae
student	myfyriwr	these	hyn
sugar	siwgr	they	nhw
suit	siwt (f)	thing	peth

this	'ma	**U**	
this	hyn	U.S.A.	U.D.A.
thousand	mil	(Unol Daleithiau America)	
three	tri (m),tair (f)	under	dan
throat	llwnc	underpants	trôns
throw	taflu	understand	deall
tick	tic (m)	unemployed	di-waith
ticket	tocyn	university	prifysgol
tie	tei (m)	until	hyd
tight	tyn	us	ni
time	amser	**V**	
tire	teiar	value	gwerth
to	i	vegetables	llysiau
toast	tost (m)	very	iawn
today	heddiw	viaduct	traphont
toilet paper	papur tŷ bach	village	pentref
tomato	tomato	**W**	
tomorrow	yfory	wake up	deffro
tongue	tafod	Wales	Cymru
tonic	tonic	want	moyn, eisiau
tonight	heno	war	rhyfel
too	rhy (a),	warm	twym
	hefyd (adv)	water	dŵr
too much	gormod	wave	ton (f),
tooth	dant		chwifio (v)
total	cyfanswm	way	ffordd
towel	tywel	we	ni
town hall	neuadd y	weather	tywydd
	dref	week	wythnos
traffic	traffig	weekend	penwythnos
train	trên (m)	weigh	pwyso
tree	coeden	welcome	croeso (m)
trousers	trowsus	Welsh	Cymraeg
trout	brithyll	Welsh	Cymreig (a)
teapot	tebot	Welshman	Cymro
two	dau (m),	Welsh people	Cymry
	dwy (f)	Welshwoman	Cymraes
		what?	beth?
		when?	pryd?

where?	ble?
which	pa
white	gwyn
will	bydd
will?	fydd?
win	ennill
window	ffenestr
wine	gwin
wink	winc (f)
with	â, gyda
without	heb
woman	menyw
wonderful	gogoneddus
wool	gwlân
work	gwaith (m), gweithio (v)
worker	gweithiwr
world	byd
worry	poeni

Y

year	blwyddyn
yellow	melyn
yes	ie, oes, ydy, oedd, bydd
yesterday	ddoe
yet	eto
you	chi, ti
your	eich, dy

Welsh interest from Hippocrene . . .

WELSH-ENGLISH/ENGLISH-WELSH STANDARD DICTIONARY

612 pages • 5 1/2 x 8 1/2 • 10,000 entries • 0-7818-0136-2 • NA • $24.95pb • (116)

TRADITIONAL FOOD FROM WALES
A Hippocrene Original Cookbook
Bobby Freeman
Welsh food and customs through the centuries. This book combines over 260 authentic, proven recipes with cultural and social history
332 pages • 5 1/2 x 8 1/2 • 0-7818-0527-9 • NA $24.95 • (638)

Other titles of interest from Hippocrene . . .

BRETON-ENGLISH/ENGLISH-BRETON DICTIONARY AND PHRASEBOOK

131 pages • 3 3/4 x 7 • 1500 entries • 0-7818-0540-6 • W • $11.95pb • (627)

BRITISH-AMERICAN/AMERICAN-BRITISH DICTIONARY AND PHRASEBOOK

160 pages • 3 3/4 x 7 • 1,400 entries • 0-7818-0450-7 • W • $11.95pb • (247)

LANGUAGE AND TRAVEL GUIDE TO BRITAIN

266 pages • 5 1/2 x 8 1/2 • 2 maps, photos throughout, index • 0-7818-0290-3 • W • $14.95pb • (119)

IRISH-ENGLISH/ENGLISH-IRISH DICTIONARY AND PHRASEBOOK

160 pages • 3 3/4 x 7 • 1,400 entries/phrases • 0-87052-110-1 NA • $7.95pb • (385)

SCOTTISH GAELIC-ENGLISH/ ENGLISH-SCOTTISH GAELIC DICTIONARY

162 pages • 5 1/4 x 4 • 8,500 entries • 0-7818-0316-0 • NA • $8.95pb • (285)

ETYMOLOGICAL DICTIONARY OF SCOTTISH-GAELIC

Alexander Macbain

There are 6,900 words discussed in this dictionary. Readers will find a pure lexicon of Scottish Gaelic, purged of the Irish words that are often thrown into dictionaries of this sort. Two thirds of the vocabulary includes native Gaelic and Celtic words; twenty percent is borrowed, and thirteen percent is of an ambiguous origin. This extensive work is founded on the Highland Society's Gaelic Dictionary.

416 pages • 5 ½ x 8 ½ • 6,900 entries • 0-7818-0632-1 • NA • $14.95pb • (710)

SCOTTISH PROVERBS

130pages • 5 ½ x 8 ½ • 25 illustrations • 0-7818-0648-0 • W • $14.95hc • (719)

Cookbooks of interest from Hippocrene...

CELTIC COOKBOOK: Traditional Recipes from the Six Celtic Lands Brittany, Cornwall, Ireland, Isle of Man, Scotland and Wales

Helen Smith-Twiddy

This collection of over 160 recipes from the Celtic world includes traditional, yet still popular dishes like Rabbit Hoggan and Gwydd y Dolig (Stuffed Goose in Red Wine).

200 pages • 5 1/2 x 8 1/2 • 0-7818-0579-1 • NA • $22.50hc • (679)

TRADITIONAL RECIPES FROM OLD ENGLAND

Arranged by country, this charming classic features the favorite dishes and mealtime customs from across England, Scotland, Wales and Ireland.

128 pages • 5 x 8 1/2 • 0-7818-0489-2 •W • $9.95pb • (157)

ENGLISH ROYAL COOKBOOK: FAVORITE COURT RECIPES

Elizabeth Craig

Dine like a King or Queen with this unique collection of over 350 favorite recipes of the English royals, spanning 500 years of feasts! Start off with delicate Duke of York Consommé as a first course, then savor King George the Fifth's Mutton Cutlets, and for a main course, feast on Quails a la Princess Louise in Regent's Plum Sauce, with Baked Potatoes Au Parmesan and Mary Queen of Scots Salad. For dessert, try a slice of Crown Jewel Cake, and wash it all down with a Princess Mary Cocktail. These are real recipes, the majority of them left in their original wording. Although this book is primarily a cookery book, it can also be read as a revealing footnote to Court history. Charmingly illustrated throughout.

187 pages • 5 1/2 x 8 1/2 • 0-7818-0583-X • W • $11.95pb • (723)

THE ART OF IRISH COOKING

Monica Sheridan

Nearly 200 recipes for traditional Irish fare.

166 pages • 5 1/2 x 8 1/2 • 0-7818-0454-X • W • $12.95pb • (335)

TRADITIONAL FOOD FROM SCOTLAND: THE EDINBURGH BOOK OF PLAIN COOKERY RECIPES

A delightful assortment of Scottish recipes and helpful hints for the home—this classic volume offers a window into another era.

336 pages • 5 1/2 x 8 • 0-7818-0514-7 • W • $11.95pb • (620)

Love Poetry from Hippocrene . . .

CLASSIC ENGLISH LOVE POEMS

edited by Emile Capouya

This lovely anthology comes in a charming gift edition and contains 95 classic poems of love from 45 poets that have continued to inspire over the years.

130 pages. • 6 x 9 • illus • 0-7818-0572-4 • W • $17.50hc • (671)

SCOTTISH LOVE POEMS: A PERSONAL ANTHOLOGY, Re-issued edition

edited by Lady Antonia Fraser

Lady Fraser collects the loves and passions of her fellow Scots, from Burns to Aileen Campbell Nye, into a book that will find a way to touch everyone's heart.

253 pages • 5 1/2 x 8 1/4 • 0-7818-0406-X • NA • $14.95pb • (482)

IRISH LOVE POEMS: DÁNTA GRÁ

edited by Paula Redes
illus. by Peadar McDaid

Mingling the famous, the infamous, and the unknown into a striking collection, these works span four centuries up to the most modern of poets such as Nuala Ni Dhomhnaill and Brendan Kennelly.

146 pages • 6 x 9 • illus. • 0-7818-0396-9 • W • $17.50hc • (70)

TREASURY OF IRISH LOVE POEMS, QUOTATIONS & PROVERBS in Irish and English

edited by Gabriel Rosenstock

This compilation of over 70 Irish love poems, quotations and proverbs spans 15 centuries and features English translations as well as poetry from such prominent Irish poets as Colin Breathnach and Nuala Ní Dhomhnaill. With selections exploring the realm of lost love, first love, and love's powerful grasp, discover why this book is essential to any Irish literature collection—and discover why "The power of poetry, coupled with the power of love, is alive and well and living in Ireland."

Gabriel Rosenstock is a noted Irish poet and translator. He wrote the Introduction to Hippocrene's bestselling *Irish Love Poems: Dánta Grá.*

128 pages • 5 x 7 • 0-7818-0644-5 • W • $11.95hc • (732)